NONPROFIT BOARDS

What to Do and How to Do It

*By John E. Tropman
and Elmer J. Tropman*

CWLA Press

Washington, DC

NONPROFIT BOARDS

What to Do and How to Do It

"And, while there's no reason yet to panic, I think it only prudent that we make preparations to panic."

CWLA Press is an imprint of the
Child Welfare League of America, Inc.

The Child Welfare League of America (CWLA) is a North American, privately supported, nonprofit, membership-based organization committed to preserving, protecting, and promoting the well-being of all children and their families. Believing that children are our most valuable resource, CWLA, through its membership, advocates for high standards, sound public policies, and quality services for children and their families in need.

CHILD WELFARE LEAGUE OF AMERICA, INC.
440 First Street, NW, Third Floor, Washington, DC 20001-2085
E-mail: books@cwla.org

CURRENT PRINTING (last digit)

10 9 8 7 6 5 4 3 2 1

Cover design by Veronica J. Morrison

Text design by Steve Boehm

Printed in the United States of America

ISBN # 0–87868–694–0

Library of Congress Cataloging-in-Publication Data

Tropman, John E.
    Nonprofit boards: what to do and how to do it / by John E. Tropman and Elmer J. Tropman.
        p.   cm.
    Includes bibliographical references (p.).
    ISBN 0-87868-694-0
    1. Boards of directors.   2. Nonprofit corporations--Management.
I. Tropman, Elmer J.   II. Title.
HD2745.T79   1999
658.4'22--dc21
                                                        98-49936
                                                          CIP

Contents

Foreword

You have heard it said. You have probably even experienced it. When many people look at the same thing, they do not all see the same thing.

Reasons for this phenomenon have been offered for centuries. One of my favorite explanations for why we perceive things so differently dates to Thomas Aquinas, the 13th-Century saint and sage. He is remembered as a theologian, philosopher, metaphysician, and physicist in an age when disciplines were not yet sharply delineated. More importantly, he was one of those gifted people who could reduce profound and complex ideas to simple levels for comprehension.

In terms of differing perceptions of the same reality, Aquinas noted that something is received according to the disposition of the receiver or, in Latin, *id quod recipitur, secundum modum recipientis recipitur.* To make his point, Aquinas filled a glass with water and observed that water takes the shape of the glass. He then applied this simple principle to human communication. Obviously, personal experiences shape our "glasses" and will play a big role in what we see or hear and how we perceive it.

Psychology assumes that individuals perceive things differently. The Rorschach test helps us assess how widely perceptions vary. Inkblots with the same shapes, but with no special meanings, are placed before different people. The people are asked to interpret what they see in the inkblots. Different people see very different things!

As common as this phenomenon is, truth be told, many things that look alike or sound alike are actually very different.

It is not always a matter of perception. Nowhere is this more evident than in the world of nonprofit organizations.

The nonprofit sector is not a monolithic reality. The term *nonprofit* describes a range of organizations differing in size, scale, and scope—from the largest and most powerful universities and foundations to the smallest and least-funded neighborhood organizations. They also vary widely in mission. Some enhance the lives of communities through the arts and humanities; others focus on problem solving through health, education, or welfare programs; still others promote civic engagement. Regardless of their differences in purpose or policy, they all have, or are expected to have, a board of directors.

All boards share common responsibilities. A board gives purpose and direction to an organization. And to the community, the board gives accountability for the organization's stated mission. Beyond these general commonalities, however, boards are not the same. They differ in composition, size, and the quality of their functioning. For good or evil, depending on the situation, a nonprofit board may not be what it seems.

Professor John Tropman of the University of Michigan and his recently deceased father, Elmer J. Tropman, a leader for more than 50 years in health and social welfare nonprofit organizations in Pittsburgh, have made a valuable contribution in narrowing the gap between what boards are and what they should be. In writing *Nonprofit Boards: What to Do and How to Do It*, the Tropmans have drawn on their many years of experience to craft a readable, usable text to strengthen the contributions of board members. Taken seriously and used well, this valuable tool can make quality performance the norm for board functioning. Though educational in purpose, this book is written in a conversational style that reflects the authors' awareness of practice as well as principle.

Nonprofit Boards is published at an important time in history. The environment for nonprofit organizations has changed in many ways. A generation ago, law suits against nonprofits were rare. Not so today. Thus, boards must be more sophisticated in dealing with organizational challenges. Risk management demands competence.

A prevailing difficulty facing many nonprofit organizations, and the nonprofit sector itself, lies in the ambiguity of their expected roles in the United States today. Our society traditionally has had three distinct sectors, each with a special purpose. Their boundaries are shifting, and ambiguity is the result. Much of the nonprofit sector's ambiguity comes from changes in the other two major sectors in this society, namely the public sector (the government) and the for-profit sector. With shifts in public policy priorities, and with a growth of for-profits in activities historically identified with nonprofits, nonprofit boards must not only be competent in the programs of their organizations, but in translating the value of these programs to the public. *Nonprofit Boards* is not a blueprint for dealing with such challenges. Nonetheless, the book focuses on strengthening the people involved to func-tion in the best possible way to deliver their programs and to overcome the challenges that come from a litigious and changing environment.

I offer a personal recollection to the readers of this book. *Nonprofit Boards: What to Do and How to Do It* reflects John Tropman's life commitment as an educator at one of the nation's finest universities. The book also reflects his lifetime opportunity to be a student of his father, who was a master at promoting civic engagement and community problem solving. For many years, Elmer J. Tropman was the executive director of the Health and Welfare Planning Association of Pittsburgh and Allegheny County in south-western Pennsylvania. As a resident of that area, I frequently had the privilege of being involved in community projects undertaken through the leadership of Elmer Tropman. Admirers of Mr. Tropman's abilities coined the term, the "Tropman touch." It designated not only efficiency in the inefficient and sticky work of community problem solving and of community development, but the knack for getting the right people to the table...and with staying power.

This book will permit another generation of nonprofit board members to enjoy the social well-being that comes from the Tropman touch!

Thomas J. Harvey
Senior Vice President of Member Services
Alliance for Children and Families
President Emeritus
Catholic Charities USA

Preface

American society, characteristically, has been oriented toward the individual and his or her achievements in the world. Perhaps for this reason we have been less sensitive to the needs and requirements of the group. Despite the fact that groups have been important to us both historically and currently, we tend to ignore and dismiss them as incompetent and lackluster. "A camel," it is said, "is a horse assembled by a board of directors."

Yet groups have many strengths different from and greater than individuals. For one thing, they correct errors by providing a plurality of perspectives. Brainstorming can get many good ideas on the table for discussion. Second, they provide social support. People need to have social support and validation for the ideas and concepts they express. Ideas are not usually presented fully formed but rather are elaborately constructed, bit by bit, by others, like a snowball rolling downhill, gaining in size as it rolls. The conceptual snowball picks up an idea here and there as it rolls along, resulting in a well-rounded concept. Then, too, groups foster competition for respect, which provides a stimulus for greater effort [Tropman, Johnson, & Tropman 1992].

Each of these strengths has its problems. Having a multitude of perspectives is not useful if people do not begin with correct information. Social support and concern for cohesion can lead to groupthink and pressures to conform [Janis 1972, 1983], and competition can result in destructive effects. Withal, though, groups today are vital to the functioning of a complex society in general, and American society in particular needs them because of our tendency to regard the individual as the most central unit.

Boards of directors are an important group in our society. They make decisions about a range of matters appropriate to their organization. They need to improve their functioning and the quality of their decisions, however [Carver 1990; Duca 1986; Houle 1989; Schmid, Dodd, & Tropman 1987; Waldo 1985; Zander 1982, 1993]. In recent years, both corporate and nonprofit boards have been taking more of a leadership role, asserting themselves, and seeking active ways to make the responsibility real to themselves and to their publics. But large questions remain: "What are boards supposed to do?" Nonprofit boards are especially needful of direction and assistance here because they most often can least afford professional help.

This book is aimed at assisting board directors and staff toward achieving this goal. Part I introduces key ideas. We cover these ideas in subsequent chapters, but for a quick overview, start here.

Acknowledgments

I would like to express appreciation to several people whose help was vital in the production of this volume.

Elmer J. Tropman, my father and coauthor, died at the end of February 1993, during the middle of this project. For obvious reasons, it was difficult to return to it. We did, however, have an initial draft, and his corrections, emendations, and suggestions inform every page. He was a United Way executive for many years and, following that, embarked on a second career as a foundation executive. He thus had long board experience; indeed, the impetus for a "board book" was originally his. A whole career of "boardship" is represented here—from the CEO's perspective as well as that of the director-member.

Working with your father is an experience in itself. During his final illness, he expressed sadness that he could not see the project to completion. I know he is joyful that it is now brought to closure, and more joyful that people can use it to help in achieving better boards and a more enhanced realization of civic purpose.

Throughout the process, many others contributed greatly. Gary McCarthy and Bob Myers made detailed comments, which were extremely useful. A special thanks is due to John Martin, former executive director of Catholic Social Services, Ann Arbor, Michigan, whose thoughtful approach to boardmanship is reflected throughout the pages.

Thanks as well go to the many "masters of boardship," who shared with us their insights and recipes about achieving excellence, quality, and high performance.

Producing a volume like this involves several drafts, which are always necessary. Without the assistance of Kathy Cornell,

Dawnine Jessen, Roxanne Loy, and Ann Page, this volume would not have been possible. They worked on the drafts and supervised the packaging, but did more—they questioned parts that were unclear, pointed to needed expansions, and noted sections that overlapped. With their help, the volume is immeasurably better. They deserve special thanks.

Dan Madaj, editor extraordinaire, not only worked through the text, but helped to smooth it. His skills with words helped the flow in countless ways. Without him, there would be no book.

Finally, I must mention my publishers and the staff of the Child Welfare League of America. Sue Brite deserves my deep appreciation for her early enthusiasm, badly needed at a time when I was working through a difficult manuscript—difficult because of my Dad's death and because it was hard to work on the text. She was so upbeat that it sustained my confidence in the project.

Then there is my editor, Steve Boehm. Steve had a tough job, taking a manuscript written originally by two people, revised by one (and over a long period of time), and making it into an attractive whole. He accomplished this task with grace, skill, understanding, and an unflagging respect for the editor-author relationship. I thank you both, and I know my Dad adds his congratulations as well.

Part I

An Introduction to the Modern Board

"Now, just a darn minute, Fowler! You're not the only member of this board who was a victim of ritual satanic abuse!"

1

Part I

An Introduction to the Modern Board

Overview

Nonprofit boards have a unique place in the structure and functioning of American society. Hundreds of thousands of voluntary organizations exist—from churches to schools and universities, from foundations to small storefront operations. In many ways, they are quite similar to for-profit organizations, but they have many differences as well. We consider here some of these similarities and differences, as well as the main responsibilities of nonprofit boards.

Chapter 1

The Differences Between For-Profit and Nonprofit Organizations

Becoming a board member is a challenge and a responsibility. So much depends on us, it seems. Whether we are talking about a profit-making organization or one that is nonprofit, the role of the member seems both unclear and yet of increasing importance. For many years, a sharp distinction existed between the for-profit *director* and the nonprofit *board member*. Happily, the executive and governance terminology of these two enterprises are becoming more similar, and the commonalties and differences better understood.

Executive Terminology

Although a great many agencies still call the highest-paid person in the organization the *executive director,* increasingly many are using the term *president.* That person may also be known as the *chief executive officer (CEO),* the *chief operating officer (COO),* or the *chief professional officer (CPO).* This is true for both for-profit and nonprofit organizations. In this book, we will use the more traditional *executive director* or simply *executive.*

The head of the board is the *chair* or *chairperson.* Those occupying seats on the board are *directors*—the for-profit terminology—which seems a bit more vigorous than the flaccid *board member.*

Organizations are writing job descriptions for both for-profit and nonprofit directors. Parties are urging evaluations of both the directors' performances and the decision stream. People involved with these organizations are paying increased attention to the need for directors to look at strategic policy matters rather than become enmeshed in administrative concerns—though there is an overlap, to be sure.

Similarities and Differences

For the most part, nonprofit and for-profit organizations are the same. Each has goals, and each seeks to maximize these goals. The fact that the goals may be different is less significant than commonly supposed.

There are some differences, however. Nonprofit organizations have a different legal status. They are exempt from taxes, in exchange for which they serve, as organizations, a civic rather than a personal purpose. How they define this civic purpose is an important question, as is how they know whether they achieve this goal. But the situation is not completely either-or. Nonprofit organizations are entitled—and indeed expected—to look after their own survival. And, although for-profit organizations serve primarily personal purposes, they also have civic duties to consider, especially when one of their products has a flaw, is tampered with, or experiences similar difficulties.

A second difference, for better or worse, is expectations. Nonprofits are often held to higher standards of behavior. This expectation extends beyond organizational purpose itself to include staff and the place of work. Office quarters cannot be plush, executive and other compensation is lower, and perks are fewer than is sometimes true in the for-profit sector. The public often thinks that the staffs of nonprofits do not need adequate pay, almost as if they were volunteering their services. This cultural construct is something that the nonprofit director and president must constantly keep in mind. Whereas for-profit organizations must keep civic purpose in mind, the nonprofit must keep personal purpose in mind and interpret its needs to itself and to the public.

Other differences exist as well. For instance, the president of a nonprofit board typically does not have a voting seat. Directors of nonprofits are outside directors—that is, they do not receive compensation from the corporation. They act as volunteers. For-profits are beginning to think that perhaps more outside directors might be a good thing. The sense, however, that volunteers have no duties and can do whatever they like is giving way, as we said, to job descriptions and evaluations.

Finally, the legal obligations of profit and nonprofit directors may be construed differently. Certainly, in both cases, following the law is such a basic injunction that one thinks it hardly needs mentioning. If the law is not crystal clear, however, differences of approach develop. For this reason, many nonprofit organizations take out liability insurance so that their directors' own personal resources will not be exposed as a result of their actions as directors. The appendix, by attorney Tom A. Croxton, details some of the considerations that nonprofit directors may want to take into account.

We mention these similarities and differences because, although this book is aimed at the nonprofit director, almost everything in it applies to the for-profit director as well.

Chapter 2

An Overview
of the Modern Board

This book presents some systematic perspectives on the modern board, which has a much more complex, intricate, and involved structure than people usually understand. Through the board, the pluralism of American values is expressed, and democratic involvement in decisions affecting individual lives is orchestrated. And then there are the regular board chores of making policy for the agency.

Despite these important large-scale social functions, as well as the crucial day-to-day decisional functions, board membership is treated casually, even shabbily. Nearly everyone involved with nonprofit organizations conspires in this casualness and shabbiness—directors who accept board positions without proper scrutiny and review; those of us who extend invitations for seats on boards in a thoughtless, offhand manner; executives who place education and training for their boards at the bottom of their lists of priorities; and society itself, which tends to undervalue group activities. Nonprofit organizations, whether they be philanthropic or human service, must receive leadership, stewardship, and trusteeship from their boards of directors if they are to survive.

Few areas of the modernization process have been as ignored as the board of directors in terms of research, training, or operating guidelines, though more materials are becoming available every day. Those who seek to learn more in this area and hone and improve it, are to be commended. It is not a job full of praise and thanks. Rather, one is likely to be greeted with indifference, ambivalence, and lack of concern.

There is a humorous story of a board training session in which someone says that ignorance and apathy are the two major enemies of board activities. One director listening to this comment looks at another and asks, "Do you think that's right?" The other director replies, "I don't know, and I don't care." That dilemma is the problem before us. This book is a small attempt to reduce apathy and ignorance.

Purposes and Concerns of Boards

Of course, all boards strive for quality decision making. And wherever the board is in its quest for quality, enhancing the results of its decision making, through improved procedures and participation, is the board's goal. But what is the subject of these decisions? The board's decisions aim at improving and enhancing the life of its organization and accomplishing that organization's mission and purpose. Board members are legal directors of the corporation; trustees of organizational purpose; and, in most cases, the final decision makers on all matters involving the organization—including those in which decisions change the purpose of the organization itself. They oversee fiscal, programmatic, and personnel activities and their integration, and they are responsible for the survival of the organization. To this end are quality decisions aimed.

American society frequently regards the individual as the superior problem solver and decision maker. For this reason, we often stress individual activity over group activity. Our service on boards of directors, therefore, is less well attended to, less well prepared for, and less thought out than our golf games or dinner parties.

If we prepared for a dinner party the way we prepare for many of our board meetings, the results of the evening's dinner would be catastrophic: "We didn't prepare any food for you because we didn't know what you would like until you got here!" Recent problems in the board room—one reads about them frequently in local newspapers—suggest that directors are not paying adequate attention to their boards' responsibilities. These difficulties stem not from intended negligence but rather from the great deal of ignorance and uncertainty that surround group activity in general and board activity in particular. What do boards do? What should they do? What are their responsibilities? What are the responsibilities of individuals within the context of a board? These questions remain largely unanswered.

The confusion of board responsibilities manifests itself in many ways. For example, people often modify the word *board*—*advisory* board, *decision-making* board, *policy* board. Such terms confuse responsibilities on the one hand with functions on the other. For our purposes here, a board of directors is a legally chartered corporation in one of the United States or Canadian provinces, and it has overall and complete responsibility for the management of the corporation it directs. What is involved in this responsibility?

Basic Responsibilities

First, of course, boards must meet legal requirements and conditions. Attorney Tom Croxton discusses these in the appendix. These requirements, however, are the absolute minimum that a board seeks to achieve. Beyond legal obligations, six responsibilities are basic and crucial:

- Becoming trustees of civic purpose
- Articulating vision, mission, and goals
- Making and overseeing policy decisions
- Selecting and evaluating the executive
- Adding entrepreneurship and innovation
- Introducing strategic planning and change

To carry out these responsibilities, the board needs some tools. One set of techniques involves the structure and culture of the board. The other set involves the board meeting itself.

How to Do It: Organization, Development, and Evaluation

- Developing the proper organization for the board
- Achieving balance—between board and executive and between internal and external focus
- Conducting training and development
- Clarifying positions within the board
- Assessment and evaluation

How to Do It: The Board Meeting

- Making quality decisions
- Holding effective meetings
- Managing decision rules

We briefly cover each topic here. Ensuing chapters develop these issues in more detail, concluding with an overall perspective on boardship.

What to Do

Too often, those of us who wind up on boards don't know what to do. People we have interviewed about governance complain that their boards—including themselves and their fellow directors—are ignorant about their responsibilities. Based on these discussions, and the writings of others, we have identified the key responsibilities of boards.

Trustees of civic purpose. The board of directors, particularly the voluntary board, represents the embodiment of a larger civic purpose and is the vehicle through which civic impulses for the betterment of the community are expressed. These are flowery phrases, surely, but they do represent something of the importance of the overall mission and role of the directors and the organization. It is because of civic purpose— as opposed to the personal—that society, through government, grants tax exemption to nonprofit entities.

Vision, mission, and goals. Boards and directors have the responsibility for positioning the agency for the future as well as the present, for tomorrow as well as today. Vision, and the shaping of organizational purpose to that vision, is a crucial board activity, one more frequently lost than not. The responsibility of the board is to articulate the organization's vision, translate that vision into a mission, and fashion goals from that mission that embody the vision and make it real. The board is also responsible for changing the vision when the time is appropriate.

Policy decisions. Policy is the vehicle through which vision and mission are effectuated. The board of directors makes policy for the organization. It is important that the board remain on the policy level. The problem of what is a policy decision and what is an administrative decision occurs frequently, and Chapter 5, on policymaking, provides useful concepts to keep policy and administration in their corners. While not micromanaging administration, the board, usually through its committee structure, must oversee the implementation of policy to some degree. Contemporary boards often fail in both the policymaking and oversight aspects of their responsibilities. They avoid decisions, making them too late or not at all. Often, they do not ask enough questions of the executive [Levy 1981; Schmid, Dodd, & Tropman 1987], and they sometimes fail to check the implementation of policies they have made.

Selecting and evaluating the executive. One of the most important responsibilities that boards have is to select the executive director of the organization and to evaluate that person on a regular basis. Too often, the first of these tasks is done poorly and the second is not done at all. Poor selection results from the fact that most boards don't select executives regularly or frequently. Hence, whatever accumulated wisdom exists about the selection process tends to be lost in the interim. The search process overall, the legal requirements that may surround it, the useful practices to follow—all are forgotten.

As we said, boards often fail to evaluate the executive director. Once they hire the executive, not much more is heard from the board until, perhaps, the executive is fired. Signals sometimes come in the form of lower or higher salary increments but cannot substitute for a sit-down, talk-through of the past year's accomplishments and problems. And the lack of evaluation experience is an additional cause of the lack of experience that boards display in the hiring process.

Entrepreneurship and innovation. Agency vitality is not manufactured by doing the same thing again and again. Rather, agencies need innovation and periodically may need to be reinvented [Naisbitt & Aburdene 1985]. Directors are responsible for changing the organization to keep it current. That is major change. But the board also needs to champion minor change—the kind of day-to-day improvements that everyone talks about but few do much about. Transforming the system and tweaking the system—both are necessary.

Strategic planning and change. Boards have a fundamental responsibility to chart the course of their organizations.

Such a process involves strategic planning. Every couple of years, the board should reassess the organization's strategic goals, adding goals if needed and removing outdated goals as appropriate. Strategic planning involves, obviously, change in the organization's missions. As important, however, strategic change also requires changes to an organization's structure. The structure of the agency needs to be aligned with its missions. As Henry Mintzberg, the famous organizational analyst, would put it, "Fit is it."

Legal obligations. As collective entities, boards have legal responsibilities under state statutes. Individual directors are responsible—ethically and sometimes legally—for the conduct of the corporation as well. The appendix addresses legal obligations in detail.

How to Do It: Organization, Development, and Evaluation

Carrying out these major responsibilities is a daunting task. Boards must organize themselves to accomplish these purposes, and there are several areas to which they must a give attention:

Board organization. Boards cannot simply "meet." They must develop structures for attending to the various aspects of the business at hand. Directing a modern nonprofit agency in a complex organizational environment requires a structure that is proper for the task. Typically, such a structure requires the board to establish committees that can deal with special aspects of the problems facing the whole board and make policy recommendations to the board.

Proper balance. This task comes in two parts. First, issues of policy and administration speak to the topic of balance between the executive and the board. The executive director has both administrative and policy roles in the organization. How the policy role is articulated is one question. In some organizations, executives are ex officio members of the board; in others, they are full members. In still others, the executive has the title of *president* and is chair of the board. As we noted in Chapter 1, this is a time of transition for executive and board responsibilities. Organizations must give careful attention to how they outline each, and they should consider cooperative templates where interests are shared.

The second half of this task entails maintaining a balance between internal and external matters. The board's internal focus involves oversight, which we have already mentioned. The external focus is attention to the environment in which it operates, to linkages and partnerships with other organizations, to changes and developments in its world. Too much looking inside results in tunnel vision—the board misses the forest of change "out there" because of preoccupation with things "in here." On the other hand, looking "out there" all the time fails to address how things "in here" are actually going. Balance is the key.

Training and development. Boards are responsible for training individual members—both new members and continuing ones—as well as enhancing the development of the board as a team of policymakers. This need calls attention to the functions of ethics, social and personal corporate behavior within the role of director, and the need to think systematically about what is appropriate social and personal behavior. Aspects of this question range from adequate preparation for meetings to the most serious questions of ethics and personal involvement. Boards are responsible for replacing departing directors, introducing new or incoming directors to the organization, training current directors, developing current directors' skills, and developing the board itself. The phrase, *a sophisticated board,* versus the phrase, *an unsophisticated board,* suggests something of the idea here. One seems knowledge-able and sure-footed in the tangle of decisions; the other lumbering and inappropriate.

Board positions. Directors have different positions on boards. Some are chairpersons; others hold such offices as treasurer, secretary, and so on; and some are simply board members. Being clear about what is required of each position is vital. Contemporary boards often prepare job descriptions for each position to improve understanding about what is involved.

Assessment and evaluation. The expectations for boards and individual directors fall into four main categories:

- the individual behaviors of directors in their various positions;
- the efficiency and effectiveness of the board as a team;
- the quality of the decisions the board makes;
- specific decisions regarding the organization's mission, and the need to continually look at that area to see if the mission is still relevant, needs updating, and so on.

Each of these categories should be evaluated annually.

How to Do It: The Board Meeting

The board works through meetings—board meetings, executive committee and other committee meetings; staff meetings (held by the executive director); and scores of other meetings. How well these meetings work is the key to how well the board works. A board cannot achieve its several purposes with awful meetings. Hence, high-quality meetings are a *sine qua non*—an absolute necessity—for effective boardship.

Making quality decisions. The board not only must make policy decisions, its decisions must be of high quality. Problems in decision making and process interfere with excellent work. Typical difficulties, such as groupthink, the "Abilene Paradox," "the boiled frog phenomenon," and the "garbage can model" are to be avoided. Chapter 14 examines these pitfalls.

Holding effective meetings. A crucial board skill—holding efficient and effective meetings—is the way in which responsibilities become effectuated. A productive board meeting is one in which relevant information is processed in a timely fashion and decisions are made. If board meetings are not productive, other areas of responsibility begin to atrophy. Directors avoid coming to meetings and then do not follow through on their assignments. Learning some rules about how to make board meetings excellent enables the director, chair, or agency executive to make quality decisions.

Managing decision rules. Boards make decisions using information on the topics in question, plus a set of decision-making rules that take into account different kinds of interests. Directors need to know what these rules are and how to orchestrate their power.

A Perspective on Boardship

Boards are crucial to the functioning of the contemporary nonprofit organization. It is imperative, therefore, that the organization's directors understand their organization's mission and their own roles and responsibilities as directors. So much of what an organization accomplishes depends on the leadership of the board and the individual directors. Often, directors do not feel that way, but it is important to say, right from the beginning, that their role is vital and central.

Overall, boards of directors and their director-members are collectively and individually responsible for achieving the social purposes that spawned their organizations in the first place. Moreover, they are responsible not only for avoiding the occurrence of bad things, but for initiating the occurrence of good and improved things. Boards seek to facilitate organizational development, to do strategic planning, and to constantly develop further ways in which the organization can flourish.

Some common problems in boards deserve special attention. Overall improvement of board performance is one element. Moving from an administrative board to a policy board is another. Chapter 19 discusses these issues and others.

Organizational excellence begins with the board. Our hope is that this book will guide board members in that journey.

Exercise 1
Grade Your Board

Consider the responsibilities of boards and the skills for better boardship. Rate your board on each (A = Excellent, B = Good, C = Average, D = Poor, F = Failure). If you are not sure, put DK ("don't know").

Basic Responsibility   *Grade*

    Meets legal requirements   ____

Regular Responsibilities

    Is a trustee of civic purpose   ____

    Articulates mission, vision, and goals   ____

Makes and oversees policy decisions   ____

Selects and evaluates the executive   ____

Is appropriately entrepreneurial   ____

Introduces strategic planning and change   ____

Skills

Maintains proper board organization   ____

Achieves executive-board balance   ____

Balances outward and inward focuses   ____

Conducts training and development   ____

Assumes proper positions for boardship   ____

Performs evaluations and assessments   ____

Make high-quality decisions   ____

Holds effective meetings   ____

Manages decisions   ____

If your board rates less than A in any category, what do you think the problem(s) is (are)?

How could these problems be solved or improved upon?

What to Do: Basic Responsibilities of Boards

"We've agreed, then, to deck the halls, but the resolution to be jolly has been tabled."

Part II

What to Do: Basic Responsibilities of Boards

Overview

As directors of nonprofits go about their business, they lack clarity about how they should be spending their time. What is the "work" of the board?

We interviewed directors and chairs who had reputations as outstanding directors to develop perspectives on the subject, synthesizing their views and using them in conjunction with the writings of others.

The result is a series of six key areas of board-governance responsibility—plus one. The "plus one" is "legal responsibility." We approach that topic in the appendix because it has technical elements, and boards and directors need to consult legal counsel in their own locations.

The six responsibilities detailed here allow boards to exceed their basic legal requirements and achieve substantive success.

Chapter 3

Boards as Trustees of Civic Purpose

The first main area of board responsibility is the role of trusteeship [Greenleaf 1973]. Trusteeship extends beyond the minimum legal requirements for avoiding law suits. The trustee holds corporate charter for the benefit of the community (as tax exemption makes nonprofit organizations "instruments" of government, as discussed in Chapter 2). This idea is implied in the term *civic group*. Trusteeship speaks to the larger issues of responsibilities and obligations and the various constituencies that must be considered.

Social Responsibilities

Although the realm of an organization's social responsibilities is, as yet, unclear and subject to much discussion and concern, the question is nonetheless pertinent whether one is talking about seat belts, toxic waste, or responsibilities to staff for adequate salaries. The nonprofit and charitable board has an impressive burden of social responsibility because of its "public" (or semipublic) role through its tax exemption. Expectations thus vary.

The issue becomes even more complex because the people and causes for which the nonprofit works almost always involve the less powerful, the disadvantaged, or the vulnerable. For example, in a board designed to promote youth services, should youth be on the board? If they cannot legally serve on the board, is an ex officio role or a youth advisory committee structure appropriate? The problems are difficult. Charitable organizations or nonprofit public benefit corporations that receive charitable contributions are responsible to donors as well as to receivers and to the community. And those responsibilities are enmeshed in organizations' larger responsibilities to society.

The concept of trusteeship means that society has delegated to a particular board the accomplishment of a civic purpose. The board must think through the way in which it conducts its business and organizes itself so it may carry out this civic purpose. Boards can take several approaches to accomplishing this. One is through the very composition of the board itself.

Trusteeship Through Board Composition

Boards are created to direct organizations in carrying out their "public benefit" responsibilities. Board membership is often approached as a way to bring resources to this commitment.

There are many approaches to creating a board. People with personal wealth who can personally contribute to an organization constitute a "money board," a prime financial resource to the agency.

Sometimes, organizations recruit people with prestige rather than, or in addition to, personal wealth to add luster, acceptance, and "class" to the board and, hence, to the agency purpose as a whole. The "prestige board" helps legitimize an agency.

Organizations sometimes seek people with knowledge and experience in a particular field. The "professional board" seeks expertise.

In some cases, those most affected by the actions of the organization in question become drivers. Hence, the "stakeholder board" or "client board." So, one question about board composition is whether one has the people one needs. And how does one know who is needed, anyway?

Some organizations try to sidestep this issue by putting everyone but Mr. Kitchen Sink on the board. This practice leads to "show boards" or "trophy boards" of 50, 60, 70, or more directors. This feeble attempt to solve the problem of membership through quantification almost always, and sooner rather than later, leaves the board membership bored! And the bigger the board, the more likely the organization is run by a small elite—sometimes an executive committee, sometimes "managing committees." One organization was ultimately run by a "noncommittee" of the most "important" people in town. Good boards seem to have 15 to 25 directors.

To accomplish trusteeship, the board itself must become the instrument of trusteeship. One way to approach trusteeship, then, is to have a board of appropriate membership and size.

Trusteeship through Community Representation

But everyone cannot be on the board, especially if the size is modest. How, then, can one create involvement on the one hand while maintaining suitable size?

As an alternative to "board stuffing," we recommend establishing a visiting committee, leadership circle, or advisory board—a larger group of people who join a circle around the board. No fee is necessary to join, just a declaration of interest. The circle can provide a broad base for testing trusteeship ideas and is the source of new directors. (See the section on recruitment later in this chapter.)

Advisory boards usually convene annually. Appointing committees from the circle can augment the strength of the board. When directors leave the board, they can join the visiting committee as emeritus directors, giving them special honor without the board losing their expertise. New members of the leadership circle can work to become future directors. Membership involves minimal participation; boards expect more reactive than proactive advisory boards.

One must make a clear distinction between a leadership circle or advisory board—which broadly represents the community and has input to the board of directors—and the board itself. This is one reason why this book usually refers to board members as *directors*, not *members*—to verbally reinforce the role that they have in law and in fact. Thus, boards achieve a balanced composition that is representative of the whole community through a two-tier structure rather than seeking to accomplish all purposes through a single-tier structure.

This two-tier structure would look something like Figure 1.

Trusteeship Through Advisory Committees and Hearings

If the board requires input from a particular segment of the community, but that segment is not represented on the board (for example, the African-American, Asian American, Latino, or elderly communities), the board can establish a special advisory committee. Developed on an as-needed basis, such ad hoc arrangements can advise the board and undertake missions at the board's request. When issues of great public

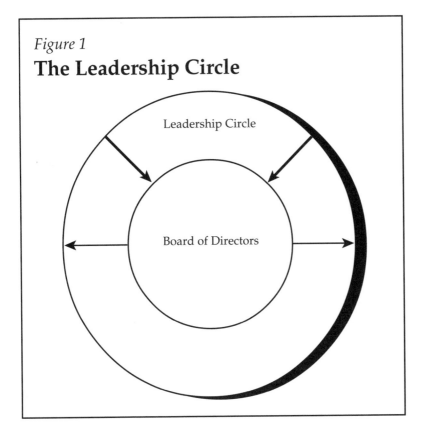

Figure 1

The Leadership Circle

Leadership Circle

Board of Directors

interest arise, the board can hold or organize public hearings, forums, or special sessions to obtain appropriate input.

Trusteeship Through Quality Participation

Boards cannot accomplish their responsibility for trusteeship with lackluster directors participating haphazardly. The criteria for board membership should be interest, competence, and a willingness to participate. Then, of course, the question of knowledge arises. Do prospective directors know what to do? Can they do it? Will they do it? Hopefully, the answer is yes. If so, board decisions are more likely to be of high quality.

Trusteeship Through Quality Decisions

One way to assess successful trusteeship is by asking if the board is making policy decisions of high quality. Although assessing the quality of a decision is difficult, doing so is important. A board is a decision-making body. Its first goal is to make decisions. Boards often do not meet this standard, or they do not meet it in a timely or honest fashion. The board that delays making decisions or that rubber-stamps executive proposals is not meeting this qualification.

Even more, the board should aim for high-quality decisions. High-quality decisions expand and enhance the board's ability to carry out the function of trusteeship. Too often, boards defer and delay decision making so long that any decision looks good to their directors, and the question of whether the decision is any good becomes beside the point. Sometimes, board discussion goes on so far into the day or night that exhaustion sets in and directors will agree to anything, good or bad. Or the executive director may sometimes bring matters to the board so close to the time when action is needed that coherent discussion is impossible, thus yielding the decision that the executive director wanted. In each case, decision quality suffers.

Recruitment as an Ongoing Process

How do boards get the people they need? The first and most obvious step is for boards to determine the capabilities they need. Boards frequently do not have visions and missions that can help provide direction here. Then there is the simple issue of finding "live bodies." Developing interested, capable directors is always a problem.

Partly because of the difficulty of the task, boards often approach recruitment as a last-minute affair. People invited to join often have no real knowledge of the agency; frequently, introductory material is not available. New directors say it can take a year or more before they know what is going on.

Boards cannot accomplish trusteeship if they are casual about recruiting. Agency visiting committees, advisory boards, or leadership circles are excellent places to begin recruiting, but boards should go beyond that. We recommend that boards keep recruitment files on an ongoing basis. Anyone can contribute to this file, and each board should assign one director—perhaps the nominating committee chair—the responsibility of keeping it updated.

When a person is nominated for directorship, the board, logically through its nominating committee, should conduct an initial interview with the candidate to determine his or her interest, time constraints, and so on, even if the potential for becoming a director is in the future. If the nominee's interest is positive, then the board can begin to gradually involve that person in the agency's affairs, during which time, both nominee and organization mutually test their fit for one another. Membership on the visiting committee should be an initial step toward directorship. A directorship should be the end of a process of involvement—it should not commence the process.

In the entire recruitment effort, the nominating committee plays a central role. That committee, one of great importance to the board, works closely with the executive director to establish a continuing list of candidates. The nominating committee continually assesses board functions and their performance to ensure a supply of interested, competent members. Recruitment must be planned, not the quick fill-the-gap approach so common today. Thus, recruitment and preparation of directors becomes a necessary rather than a sufficient condition for successful trusteeship.

Trustees of Civic Purpose

Nonprofit directors serve as trustees of civic purpose. This trust is complicated, because what the community wants is not always clear. But the nature and structure of the organization itself should be such that diverse and evolving areas of community concern can express themselves. In the next chapter, we will look at the articulation of specific visions, missions, and goals and the development of strategic and tactical approaches to accomplishing them. But without a trusteeship structure, decisions about these elements are likely to be warped and even self-serving.

Exercise 2

Try to define the concept of trusteeship for your board.
- What kind of job are you doing in the trustee-ship role?
- What kind of job is the board doing as a whole?

Do you have one of the special kinds of boards mentioned?
- Money board
- Status or prestige board
- Professional board
- Stakeholder or client board
- Trophy board

How can you move toward a more "trusteeship" structure?

What steps does your board follow in spotting potential members? Can the process be improved?

Think of establishing a two-tier community representative system as a way to achieve better representation (a visiting committee, advisory board, or leadership circle). Could you do it? Why or why not? Do you already have something like this in place?

Chapter 4

Articulating Vision, Mission, and Goals

The board is responsible for articulating a vision for the organization. Once the vision is complete, then the board can derive a more specific mission from it. Expressing a mission leads to a strategic plan and then to annual plans.

Vision and Mission

Vision embodies and expresses the hopes and aspirations that form the core of the organization's *raison d'être*—its reason for existing. It speaks of the longing for accomplishment, rather than accomplishment itself. An organizational vision is usually a short phrase: "helping teenage mothers" or "reducing domestic violence in the tri-county area." Organizations sometimes express their visions in their names and in logos or symbols (including colors) that identify and reinforce their overall missions. Organizations may also have mottos that seek to capture the essence of the agencies.

Involving everyone in creating visions, names, mottos, and logos can be exciting and motivational [Tropman & Morningstar 1989]. We urge some caution, however: Boards must anticipate and be prepared to manage conflict in participants' understanding of vision. Boards must also recognize that involving everyone calls for broad representation of all stakeholders, including staff, clients or customers, and the community in which or on whose behalf the organization operates. All should be part of this conversation.

Whereas the vision is a phrase, the mission statement is a paragraph, or at least a complete sentence, expressing in detail the areas in which the vision operates. Some sample vision and mission statements appear at right.

Strategic Plan

Vision and mission are timeless. They remain current and endure over time, until the board decides to change them. The strategic plan, however, is time limited—usually two to five years—and stipulates the specific areas in which the agency works and the programs it offers. Strategic plans are vital because each program should become a division or department of the agency (and a committee of the board, as we will see in Chapter 9). Most agencies find 3 to 10 areas of service to be about right; 5 or 6 seem to be the average. Too few, and the agency is monolithic; too many, and the agency can't remember what it is doing.

Boards have to encourage their own members and the organizations they oversee when it comes to strategic planning. Many people say, "Plans are too rigid. Let's just play it by ear." A plan is just that—a plan. It doesn't have to be carved in stone. If the environment changes, so can the plan. Think of the process as dynamic and changing, not fixed [Mintzberg 1994]. Planning requires constant establishment and alteration of direction. In this dynamic context, strategic planning is helpful and necessary. The virtue of strategic planning is the thinking and exploration that goes into it.

Sample Visions and Missions

Organization 1

Name: HELPMOM **Logo:**

Motto: The Future of Kids Is Moms

Vision: Helping Teenage Mothers

Mission statement: HELPMOM works with pregnant teenagers around issues of their own health and the health of their babies, marital and partner relationships and arrangements, and housing.

Organization 2

Name: SafeHome **Logo:**

Motto: Conflict Kills—Peace Saves

Vision: Reducing Domestic Violence in the Tri-County Area

Mission statement: SafeHome advocates and trains for nonviolent mechanisms for managing conflict in the home and provides "cool houses" for individuals before they begin violent episodes. We also provide harbor homes for victims and their families.

Annual Plan

By outlining the agency's goals and activities for the coming year, the annual plan further specifies the strategic plan: "This year we are going to do these things." Measurable goals are attached to each element.

Most boards do not think they approve an annual plan, when in fact almost all do. It is called "the budget." Unfortunately, many organizations discuss their goals by way of the budget or through arguing about allocations. In fact, discussion of the annual plan should come before the budget discussion. The budget discussion is just an instrument to accomplish goals. One might as well discuss goals directly.

Implementing Vision, Mission, and Planning

Developing these elements is one thing. Implementing them is another. Much of the rest of this book deals with how to accomplish implementation. It is important to say here, however, that implementation is greatly assisted by the "deliverables" that appear as goals in the annual plan and the strategic plan. This allows boards to check progress and make adjustments, if necessary.

Vision, mission, strategic plans, and annual plans represent important policy decisions by the board. This process is the first aspect of trusteeship through quality decisions. Quality decisions cannot be made in a haphazard, catch-as-catch-can manner. The board needs a coherent, understandable organizational plan for its mission; and the organizational structure and allocation of effort must then be broken down into components that achieve that mission. As crises arise, they can be considered within the framework of the organizational vision, mission, and strategic and annual plans.

Exercise 3

Does your agency have

- a vision statement?
- a motto?
- a logo?
- a mission statement?
- a strategic plan?
- an annual plan?

If so, are they up to date ?

If not, why not?

If not, what can your board to do get them under way?

Chapter 5

Boards as Policymakers

Policymaking is the vehicle of board action. But making good policy is not an easy task. It is not always clear what level of decisions boards should focus upon. This leads to a consideration of the policy-administration dichotomy.

Policy and Administration

The role of the board extends beyond policymaking to overseeing policy implementation as well. The line dividing policy functions from administrative functions is always unclear. We prefer the idea of intersecting sets illustrated in Figure 2 on page 43.

Differentiating policy from administration is never easy, and the separation will always be controversial. Directors should try to stay in the policy areas, however. Imperfect though the distinction may be is, the following lists should help keep things straight.

Policy functions are generally those decisions that
- have broad scope and implication,
- commit the organization's personnel or resources in a substantial way,
- are hard to reverse,
- are precedent setting, and
- have force over long periods of time.

Administrative functions are generally those decisions that
- are relatively narrow in scope and implication,
- involve reversible commitments,
- tend toward the application of precedent rather than its establishment, and
- have force over relatively short spans of time.

Clearly, these elements can be hard to differentiate.

Precisely because of their longer-range implications, policy decisions require oversight. Many aspects of a major policy decision require other subsidiary decisions to put the intent of the policy into practice. Board involvement is necessary here, in cooperation with administration, to execute policy. Without understanding the need for board oversight, executives may well resent their boards; without understanding the need for executive involvement, boards may in turn resent executives' intrusion into policy matters. There is no completely clear demarcation between policy and administration. Relationships between executives and boards are worked out to the satisfaction of both from organization to organization.

The gray area includes those issues that involve policy and administration at once or in which the amount of either is unclear. Typically, these issues become the province of the executive committee and are hashed out there before being allocated to the board as a whole or to the executive director.

Review and Refurbishment

Boards should stay in the policy area. They should make decisions. In addition to decision making, however, there is decision "remaking." This not redundancy; rather it is a policy review and refurbishment. Every five to seven years, the board should take in-depth looks at its mission, role, and

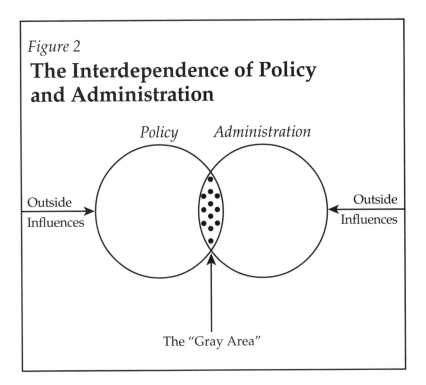

Figure 2

The Interdependence of Policy and Administration

Policy *Administration*

Outside Influences →

← Outside Influences

The "Gray Area"

articles of incorporation to ascertain whether changes in direction are necessary. Each year, the board should select one specific area of the agency-board relationship for review and, hopefully, refurbishment and improvement. The overall quality of policy decisions should be audited yearly. Thus, the board might scrutinize personnel policy one year, financial policy in another year, and so on. At the end of this five- to seven-year cycle, the board will have reviewed all of the subparts of the organization. Frequent evaluation regarding satisfaction with board meetings, and yearly assessments of decision quality, when combined with policy review and refurbishment and supplemented with information from the program audits, provide a useful overview of the organization's activities. These reviews can be accomplished during an annual one- or two-day retreat or at a special meeting in which people can look at the agency and, in doing so, reconsider their own roles in the organization.

Review and refurbishment is longer-range than the yearly assessments. Perspective and point of view are multi-year. Simply taking yearly evaluations and then looking at everything at the end of a longer period is both too little and too much. Yearly evaluations combine with the more intensive "sector" analyses when one is looking at the overall agency mission and role in the five- to seven-year review cycle. Chapter 8, on strategic change, introduces detailed information on the overall process of change.

The Budget

Approval of the budget is one of the most important elements of the board's action. Money and its care are the heart of fiduciary responsibility. Through the budget, the board implements the annual plan—and, by implication, the strategic plan, the mission, and the vision statement—by assigning portions of the agency's budgetary resources to its programmatic components. The board decides approximately how much of organizational resources should go toward accomplishing particular objectives. Ideally, boards should make these assignments regardless of the revenue generated by particular components.

Consider, for example, an agency with two central components—counseling and residential care. The board of directors might decide to spend 60% of resources on counseling and 40% on residential care. This decision permits budget makers and other policy people within the organization to draw up a budget consistent with that general directive. The income from counseling and the income from residential care may not match the proportions of effort the organization wishes to spend on them. Residential care may be generating more income than counseling, or counseling may bring in more revenue than what the board decides to budget for it. In that case, the amount of subsidy that one program requires and the other program provides is clear.

The degree of outside fundraising is also clear, and the extent to which support from outside sources must be channeled to one function or another becomes more apparent. One can simply extend this example to an agency with four or five functions, and the budget proportion allocation gives the board an opportunity to look at the various functions, assess the way in which those functions are helpful to the organization, and assign proportions of effort represented in dollar amounts to the range of functions. The Index of Dissimilarity, discussed in Chapter 13, is a way to assess how close an organization is to where one wants it to be.

Operations Audit

Quality operations are hard to assess, but it is important that the board look at the agency's operations at the end of the year. An operations audit simply examines the performance of the organization to see if the components of the annual plan have, in fact, been achieved, or, if not, why not. The board makes appropriate adjustments in the plans, targets, and goals— or personnel and other internal organizational elements—to more successfully accomplish those goals in the coming year.

The operations audit is good not only for what it does— review and adjustment—but also for what it signals, because employees of the organization are aware that, given a set of organizational missions and roles, and five-year and annual plans, there will be some accountability about the extent to which they have moved toward those goals. Particularly in the human service field, accountability is often lacking.

Some techniques appear in Chapter 13, but a few points about cost and profit centers and program financing are worth mentioning here.

In the cost-and-profit-center concept, the board and executive look at what areas of the agency are making money (areas of profit) or losing money (areas of subsidy). There is nothing wrong with either—a sliding-scale fee-for-service program, for example, might well be in the red by design. The important thing is that board and executive are aware of this.

Program financing often comes up in areas of subsidy (departments in the red) and with new proposed programs. In our experience, executives often give more planning thought to programs than to funding. This should not be surprising. Thinking up new ideas is often a lot more fun than thinking about ways to pay for them. And indeed, one wants to avoid bottom-line mentality, in which every new thing is initially judged against criteria that the new idea cannot meet simply because it is new. Hence, there may be good reasons why an organization should start or subsidize a program, and the board may not disagree. What may be at issue, however, is how to pay for it.

Decision Assessment

Evaluating policy decisions is a key policy action. Chapter 13 gives a range of techniques for approaching this, and we make a few overall comments here.

One of the most important initial steps in evaluating policy decisions and being accountable for them is to make decisions in the first place. All too often, when a problematic decision area arises, people are unaware that they made a particular decision, and upon scrutiny of the records, the time and the reason for the decision are unclear.

Most likely, the decision was not made at any one point but rather evolved at several points over time—as if one contracted separately with six architects to design a piece of a house that was then assembled by one builder. When you see the final house, you think, "My God, how did we get this?" At the end of the year, or whenever appropriate, one should be able to go back and not only answer the question, "What decisions did we make during the year?" but also review the impact, structure, and quality of those decisions overall.

Because it can be difficult to assess the impact of a decision immediately after the decision is made, such a retrospective assessment is essential to accountability. Sometimes, the wisdom or foolishness of a decision emerges only after the passage of time. An accountability review also takes into consideration the extent to which the information available at the time of the decision was sufficient and accurate. If an organization continually makes decisions that prove to be unsound, it should study very carefully how it gathers information and considers alternatives.

The decision audit or autopsy is a useful device. We detail the specific procedures for decision autopsies in Chapter 13.

The idea of a decision audit and autopsy implies a careful review of the decisions made and an assessment or judgment about whether they were successful. Clearly, those involved in decision making will quickly notice that the result of a successful decision requires two interrelated elements—a high-quality decision to begin with, and good implementation. An outstanding decision can be ruined by lousy implementation. An awful decision can be tempered, and even made to look good, by creative and brilliant implementation. In any review process, directors should look carefully at both of these aspects. They should never assume that because an outcome was positive, the decision was correct; or because the outcome was wrong, the decision was wrong. Rather, directors should look at the decision process separately from implementation.

The Policymaking Responsibility

Policy decisions are the central feature of the organization. Improving them is a key responsibility of directors. Essential to developing quality policy is an ongoing process of developing and reviewing goals. Without constant examination, organizational ennui quickly sets in.

Exercise 4

Consider your board's recent decisions. Can you locate them here?

- Policy matters
- Policy-administration (gray area) matters
- Administrative matters

Are you working in the proper areas? Why or why not? How can you improve?

Has your board developed a plan for policy review and refurbishment? If not, why not? How can the board begin one?

Has substantive program discussion preceded the budget discussion? Why or why not? How can you improve?

Do you have an operations audit in place? If not, how can one be set up?

Do you know where the cost and profit centers are in your agency? If not, how can you begin to find them?

Do you evaluate your board's decisions? If not, how could you begin?

Chapter 6

The Board as Selector and Evaluator of the Executive

Another key board responsibility, and one that is often problematic, is the search and evaluation process for the executive director. There are several common problems.

First, the search process doesn't happen very often. Many directors don't do "search and hire" in their daily lives as regularly as they do some of the other things their board roles require. Hence, their knowledge of the process is low.

Second, selecting one candidate from among many involves inherent interpersonal problems, as well as the problems of evaluation, which involve agency criticism or redirection. None one likes to receive criticism, and most of us don't like to give it either. Yet the health of the board, the health of the organization, and the ability of the board and the organization to accomplish their goals depends on good hiring and the executive's supervision.

Improving these functions requires attention to three areas. The first is the set of considerations and policies that deal with these matters. The second is the specific process that one goes through to hire an executive—the search process. The last involves specific techniques for accomplishing the evaluation process. An overview of the search process appears on page 53.

Considerations and Policy in Executive Search and Review

The whole process of executive search and review can be simpler if directors attend to a few matters first. Among the more important is setting up a contractual period for which the executive is to be hired. Three to six years is a good range. If directors want a longer time period, then the board should undertake a specific major evaluation of the executive midway through the contract period, and it should write this requirement into the contract. The board should already plan to evaluate the executive annually, specifying the procedures in the contract. Being this specific is important—establishing positional procedures is always easier when no one is in the position yet. Candidates are then aware of these requirements as they interview for the position.

Too often, executives stay because no one knows how to get rid of them. Executive turnover is less often due to incompetence or bad performance than to organizational changes in goal structure and direction, or an executive's desire for a larger, smaller, or different role. Most everyone recognizes that people have different skills. Not infrequently do the skills of a particular executive meet an organization's needs at a specific point in time but not at another. The board needs ways to assist that executive to move to a job where his or her skills are more appropriate and to secure someone who has the skills for this phase of the agency's development and activity.

One way to do this is to link the executive's term to the major policy review and refurbishment schedule. If the organization undertakes a major assessment every seven years,

Steps in the Search Process: Finding Top Staff

✎✓ Vacancy appears or will appear.

✎✓ Review mission and goals.

  ✏ ❐ Reaffirm goals.

  ✏ ❐ Establish search policy and protocol.

  ✏ ❐ Establish staff, funding, and other necessary resources.

✎✓ Appoint CEO assessment committee.

✎✓ Post the position, based on review of mission and goals.

✎✓ Seek candidates as well as accept applications.

✎✓ Review written materials; review references.

✎✓ Prepare short list.

✎✓ Interview, using questions based on search policy and protocol.

✎✓ Rank candidates.

✎✓ Make an offer; be open to negotiation.

this could be when goals are readjusted. Tying the executive's contract to that schedule makes it possible for the agency to change executive directors, if necessary, consistent with a change in the organization's goals. Without such a connection, the change in the agency's direction may not occur, even though the board has approved a formal change in mission.

Directors must also be aware of legal requirements regarding the hiring of a new executive. Some of these requirements may be specified in the organization's bylaws and may detail specific procedures for search and selection. Other laws may also govern the search process.

Agencies can often secure help with both search and assessment from national organizations or specialized search firms. For example, United Way of America and United Way of Canada both assist local United Way chapters in the search process; conferring with representatives of these central organizations may be useful before directors set about selecting a new executive.

The Selection Process

The selection process itself is complex and has many steps. The process begins when the agency determines it has a vacancy, and continues until it announces a final selection. Because organizations engage in this process so rarely, they often handle it poorly. They must take special care to proceed thoughtfully, rationally, and systematically.

The overall sequence of steps is straightforward—decide on the search criteria, advertise the position, narrow candidates to a short list, interview those on the short list, and make a final selection. Several specific difficulties are worth considering.

Search policy. What are the criteria? What is the timeline for making a final selection? What is the salary range? How will the organization respond to secondary issues, such as the career of the spouse? Talk about all of this ahead of time, before announcing the position. A consultant can be very helpful.

Search committee. Who should be on the search committee? Should it be a committee of the whole, a specially elected committee of the board, the nominating committee, or the executive committee? We recommend using an augmented executive committee—the officers of the organization, the chairs of the other major committees, plus one or two members specially elected at large. This gives breadth and depth to the selection process. The search committee chair should be someone other than the board president, because the president will have enough ongoing responsibilities. The board can hold a special election to fill any of these positions on the search committee.

Staff assistance. What kind of person should the board select to provide staff support? It has to be someone with access to the organization's mechanical resources—such as word processors and the photocopier—as well as someone who is sufficiently knowledgeable about the organization. Sometimes, the outgoing executive serves this role. Other times, the board may want to secure an outside person for this task or use a consultant or search firm. If there are internal candidates for the executive's position, be careful that they do not exercise undue influence or are unduly neglected.

More and more organizations are using "head hunter" or search firms. These firms have several advantages. They often have specialists in the specific areas where agencies need assistance. Because their people make a lifetime of this kind of work, they bring a wealth of savvy to the task. But their experience does not come cheap.

Money for the search. Is this to be a national or a local search? Will the search committee bring in candidates from out of town for interviews, or will it conduct such interviews by telephone? Sometimes, the committee may want to visit candidates. The search committee will have to work out overall procedures and make arrangements with the organization for a special budget line so the committee knows what it has to work with.

Rewards for the candidate. The cost of the search itself is not the only budgetary item that needs consideration. What is the salary range of the job and its possible perquisites? For example, is the agency willing to pay moving expenses for an out-of-town candidate, or provide a car? Boards often fail to consider such questions until candidates bring them up.

Vision and mission. Many search committees flounder immediately because someone says, "I can't look for anyone until I know exactly what we're going to ask that person to do." That sounds reasonable on the surface, but it has the seduction of a half-truth. Certainly it is important for the organization to have a set of general expectations for the new executive. These expectations may even be written down in a job description. It is equally true, however, that most organizations hope that the executive will assist in defining the mission and role of the organization and that he or she will give vigor and vitality to that process. In the back of people's minds is the notion that if the job is defined too specifically, the most interesting applicants won't take it. Who wants to simply carry out the detailed instructions of others? Hence, the board should develop a general statement, but it should be an "open statement"—not overly detailed, but something that will give candidates and the search committee a sense of the agency's mission and interests. The statement should also convey the board's expectation that the candidate will contribute materially to the agency's mission and vision.

Proactivity and reactivy. The search committee must be balanced between proactivity and reactivity, between invitation and response. Many committees take the view that they will post a job; interested candidates will apply; and, from that applicant pool, one will be selected. This view is only partly accurate. While the search committee is looking over the potential executive, she or he is looking them over. The assessment and interview process is always a two-way street. Search committees must both assess and recruit the potential candidate. The archives of boards of directors are filled with sad stories about "the one who got away"—the perfect person who, in the final analysis, was not interested, often because of hostile treatment (sometimes called "tough questions") by the search committee. We do not mean to suggest that search committees should avoid asking "tough questions," rather that questioning not come off as antagonistic, off-putting, or unwelcoming.

At least initially, search committees should not be too rigid about who is and who is not a candidate. The committee may ask someone to apply, but that person may already have a good job and no initial interest in applying. The committee may have to "create" an interest. Too, the idea of "applying" makes some potential candidates feel like applicants, and they perceive themselves to be at a disadvantage. In such cases, the search committee may find it useful to invite those candidates to "explore possibilities" with the committee. This can be informal discussions in which the individual begins the process as a "consultant" to the organization—regarding the agency's future, for example. During initial discussions, the search committee can scrutinize the extent of the candidate's abilities in a more tranquil atmosphere and explore the extent of the consultant's potential interest somewhat more diplomatically. The committee must be open to explore possibilities with a range of people and a range of positions, at least during the early stages of its search.

Look, look, look! Most search committees sit and wait for applicants to approach them. It is important to identify strong potential candidates and approach them—ask them about their interests, invite their applications or consultation—and produce a solid list of candidates. Veterans of the search process know to expect the unexpected. The best candidate, the candidate of choice, may drop out at the last minute for personal reasons. When that happens, the agency, which has relied heavily on that candidate, has to start its search all over again.

Keep candidates informed. Maintaining an equitable and informative process is vital for both the candidates and the board. Once the board decides about its overall time schedule and search procedures and begins the process, it should keep candidates abreast of developments in the search. Candidates who are clearly not in contention should be told so quickly. A more difficult situation arises when the search committee develops its so-called short list, selecting three or four top candidates and then making a choice from among them. Often, the search committee will want to avoid rejecting the other two or three people on the short list until the first choice decides what he or she is going to do. There may be no good solution to this problem. Many committees hesitate to inform candidates that they are not the first choice, but leaving candidates without any information until some distant endpoint is not satisfactory either.

In the final analysis, the board and its search committee should remain in contact with all candidates throughout the search. Many times, candidates never learn the disposition of their applications. Unbelievable as that may seem, once they makes their selections, search committees forget about the other candidates. Few organizational activities rival the lack of courtesy that often attends the search process.

These points do not cover all of the difficult areas inherent in the search process, but they do touch upon some of the more common ones. Perhaps what is most important is for the search committee to put itself in the applicants' shoes. That will give the committee a more realistic idea of the nature and sequence of its questions and search procedures. And it suggests the kind of treatment that might be appropriate.

Review and Assessment

The search process can set the stage for the process of evaluation. Earlier, we suggested that an evaluation policy be in place specifying a contract period and requiring regular evaluations. Holding such evaluations annually may prove most useful, although other time periods may be more appropriate to particular organizations. The important point is for the board to sit down with its executive and discuss accomplishments and failures during the year. This process is easier if there are two steps rather than one.

A system that works well is for the board to begin the evaluation process by discussing with the executive his or her organizational goals for the coming year. These should be operationalized or applied versions of the agency's larger mission statement and its annual goals and should represent agreed-upon directions and activities for the organization and the executive. Often useful is for the president to ask the executive to prepare a list of achievements that he or she hopes to accomplish in the coming year and to outline how they track with organizational problems and strengths. The board or its executive committee should review this memorandum, accept it or revise it, and usually talk with the executive about it. Out of that discussion should develop mutually agreed-upon activities for the year. This is important, because the executive's accomplishments depend, in large part, on the actions of others, including the board itself. Hence, the board needs to be aware that insisting on some objectives for an executive might require their involvement in a variety of ways, and they have to be prepared to commit those resources.

In any event, the board and the executive agree on a document, which provides the basis for assessment at year's end. Often, the president will sit down with the executive and go over the list of goals, covering the successes and the problems. Prior to the evaluation meeting, the board may ask the executive for a self-assessment, and the president and the board may prepare their own assessment, using the same form. When the president and executive meet, they can compare these two assessments and discuss commonalties and differences.

Boards might use other approaches to evaluation, but this two-step process of establishing targets and measuring progress toward those targets is among the better ones. The point is to have a system and to use it annually.

Termination

The whole process of search and review is designed to prevent the need to terminate the executive. Termination represents a failure of processes like those we have been discussing. Frequently in such cases, expectations and problems are not communicated. Sometimes, executives not only receive no feedback, the board lies to them: "Everything looks great." Privately, however, the board is upset and angry. The final result is termination.

Organizations can avoid such problems with thorough review and discussion. Regular, frequent meetings take the sting out of one big blockbuster session. Executives do leave, but boards should work toward and help executives find a proper fit.

Firings sometimes should and do occur. At these times, feelings run high, alternatives seem few. The best course here is to use performance reviews and specific, attainable goals and rely on the written record. It is not a case of how someone feels, but what someone has done, or not done, that is important.

Regular reviews of the executive mean that goals and objectives can be specified. Then, the board can talk with the executive about whether those goals have been.

Minimizing the Difficulties

The hiring, evaluation, and termination processes are difficult. No amount of procedure, structure, or rules can make them easy or can remove the tension, uncertainty, and complexities that arise from them. Those difficulties can be minimized, however, and one of the board's more important roles is to handle these matters with dignity and dispatch.

Exercise 5

Review the system your board uses to evaluate the executive director.

- Is there a system in place?
- Is it satisfactory?
- Does it conform to the ideas suggested here?
- How could it be improved?

Chapter 7

The Entrepreneurial Responsibility of Boards

Talking about the importance of entrepreneurial activity for boards may seem strange. Such activity is traditionally thought of as profit making and focused on small business. Nonetheless, entrepreneurship really focuses on the development of new ideas and their introduction into ongoing systems [see, for example, Tropman & Morningstar 1989]. We describe in this chapter four types of boards—the conservative board, the traditional board, the entrepreneurial board, and the "overboard"—as examples of organizational styles. Each style has its problems, but the entrepreneurial board holds the greatest promise for a vigorous, up-to-date agency.

The Conservative Board

Exemplified by a narrow-minded focus on doing things as they always have been done, the conservative board, unfortunately, has characterized many American business and agency enterprises in the latter half of the 20th Century. Conservative boards tend to regard as wise those things that are old and unwise those that are new, independent of detailed specific examinations of the "things" in question. The famous "not invented here," which has characterized many companies, has also characterized many human service boards: "We cannot use this or that procedure because we didn't develop it." Although a certain amount of conservatism is

appropriate, if an entire board is characterized by conservatism, it will not recognize opportunities in the environment
in which it operates. Hard as it is to believe, we are aware
of agencies, serving particular ethnic or cultural groups,
that have failed to notice that the ethnic groups they serve
have left! The agencies now own physical facilities sur-
rounded by people who don't need the services that the
agencies have to offer and are unable to offer the services that
their communities desire. Conservatism is an excellent perspective as long as it involves selective attention rather
than keeping everything as it has been.

The Traditional Board

The traditional board is perhaps most common in human
service agencies today. It is characterized by a hold-the-line
mentality. Change, while not opposed as in the conservative
board, is only approached over a long period of time, very
gingerly and with great difficulty. The traditional board wants
to keep an even course: "If it ain't broke, don't fix it." Traditionalism, of course, like conservatism, has its virtues. If traditionalism is so strong, however, that it drives out innovation, then it becomes problematic for the organization.

The traditional board or traditional set of directors often
develops out of—and has, over time, become captured by—
the history of the organization. Clearly, many social agencies
were developed to meet particular needs at particular times.
Many have distinguished histories of service to their communities. Nonetheless, agency services, like corporate products,
require change and updating from time to time.
Overcommitment to tradition leads to a stability that presages
decline. A certain focus and centering of agency attention are

key to an agency's identification and prestige, but environments, needs, and problems are constantly changing.

Perhaps the most dramatic example of this is the National Foundation for Infantile Paralysis, originally developed to provide aid to victims of polio. The organization faced a crisis when polio vaccines came on the market. The agency had a sound reputation, a solid national volunteer base, offices, equipment, and all the requisites to do an important job. The only problem was that its "job" was now gone. It was able to refocus its efforts on closely related children's services and continued to flourish.

For many organizations, however, change does not come in such a dramatic form. Rather, it creeps up on them. Traditional organizations must be aware that, although slow, change is present. The ability to adapt is therefore a prime requisite for organizational health. Directors have the final responsibility for asking the probing questions, tackling the challenges, and questioning historic strategic directions.

Because traditional boards are not opposed to change, they are often willing to consider change if the issue is somehow raised forcefully. In this respect, agencies with conservative boards are in worse shape than those with traditional ones. The conservative board may wish to retain traditional perspectives, operations, and trajectories at all costs. Many of these agencies wind up being "defunded" as community priorities and those of government and foundation funders shift over time.

The traditional board, however, is willing to consider new directions and new initiatives. Its problem is only that it moves too slowly and too tardily in these directions. All too often, its approach to change is more happenstance then not. If the board happens to have someone interested in and committed to organizational change and development, that "champion" might lead the board in a process of strategic planning and strategic development. If, however, such an individual champion is not present, then the kind of development referred to here might well not occur. The traditional board, unlike the entrepreneurial board, does not make organizational change and development an ongoing part of its enterprise.

The Overboard Board

Sometimes, a board of directors manifests difficulties at the other end of the spectrum from conservatism and traditionalism. These boards might be called "overboards." They often appear chaotic and unfocused. They swing from topic to topic, from issue to issue, without any overall sense of strategic or tactical direction.

The overboard board undertakes corporate-level action in a preemptory and premature way. The overboard is preemptory because it often does not think through or study particular courses of action. Innovation, while new, does not have to be sloppy. Similarly, the overboard may try to innovate prematurely, without bringing along those individuals involved and working through some of the issues and difficulties that might be involved.

The overboard is often full of strong personalities who are full of themselves, and it is frequently laced with personal conflicts among directors, between directors and the executive, and even between board and staff. The overboard board frequently identifies itself as opposite of, and therefore better than, the conservative board. Unfortunately, the organizational chaos and about-faces that characterize the overboard make it impossible for the staff to develop any kind of cohesive, coherent perspective on the job that the agency is expected to do, and their place within that job. The tragedy is that the overboard board, in its own but different way, is as troublesome and difficult as the conservative board. Never changing and always changing have similar dysfunctional impacts, although the mechanisms through which these impacts occur are different. Whereas the conservative board needs to lighten and loosen up, the overboard board needs structure and focus.

The Entrepreneurial Board

The entrepreneurial board focuses on reinventing the agency and establishing change and innovation as an ongoing part of the organization's activities. The face it presents to the community is not one of "We have always done things this way and are continuing to do them," but rather, "We are innovative and changing to meet new needs." Some of these new programs may seem strange from a traditional or conservative perspective, as in the case of a hospital director who decided to market pies and cakes from the hospital's cafeteria [Margolis 1989]. This was an entrepreneurial idea. Whether it was a good idea is less important than the fact that the director made the attempt.

Typically, the concept of entrepreneurship is associated with making money in a small business enterprise. A closer reading of the entrepreneurial literature, however, suggests that the concept has a more valid association—one involving the development of new ideas and their ongoing implementation regardless of context [Tropman 1984; Tropman & Morningstar 1989]. Hence, entrepreneurship can be used within the government agency, the advisory committee, the nonprofit agency, and the agency board, as well as the commercial enterprise.

Nor is size is requisite for entrepreneurship. Both small and large organizations require entrepreneurship, just as social agencies and commercial business do. The large public organization or welfare department requires new ideas and new approaches as much as the smaller human service organization. The concept, therefore, is not limited and narrow, but broad and useful, applying as it does to a wide range of enterprises.

So the entrepreneurial human service board makes development and implementation of new ideas an ongoing part of its regular operation. Too many boards, especially conservative and traditional ones, spend most of their time reviewing what is already happening in their organizations, checking and overseeing to be sure that nothing has gone wrong. Some portion of this activity often involves questioning the executive director, president, and staff members as to why certain events occurred. Such activity is a necessary part of any board meeting, and we will explain how to facilitate that in Chapters 15–17 on effective board meetings.

The Rule of Sixths, which we will discuss again in Chapter 16, is a good technique for that discussion. It suggests that only a fraction of the board's activity should be spent dealing with items from the past. If more than one-sixth of its time is spent on old business, it is not dealing with current and future items. About four-sixths (or two-thirds) of the items in the board meeting should be current, here-and-now activities that need board judgment and direction. Especially important for entrepreneurial considerations, the final one-sixth should be "blue sky" items—those issues for the future. It is here where anticipatory thinking takes place, when the directors seek to understand the nature of the environment in which their organization operates; recognize the changes that are developing around them; consider the new kinds of services and programs that the agency might offer, such as the hospital director's idea for marketing pies and cakes from the hospital cafeteria; and stimulate and inspirit the organization to be at the forefront of developments, encouraging proactivity rather than reactivity.

The entrepreneurial board must consistently reinvent the agency. Introduced by Naisbitt and Aburdene [1985], this concept refers to the need to reconfigure, recast, reformat, and redo agency services to meet a changing environment. Unlike the traditional board, with the occasional attempt at innovation, the entrepreneurial board makes change an ongoing part of its regular activities. Attention to innovation in the entrepreneurial board is a regular feature. Each meeting typically deals with some innovative aspect—for example, a new kind of therapeutic intervention, a new office design, a new policy. These innovations needn't be big. Rather, it is the culture of innovation that the board is stimulating by these activities. To do something well, one must do it regularly. One cannot play a musical instrument superbly, cook an exquisite meal, or give an outstanding talk only on occasion. One must perform, cook, or speak regularly. Excellence is based on regularity and repetition, until it becomes, as with a tennis player or a golfer, embedded in our "muscle memory" and neither the organization nor the athlete need think about doing it.

The entrepreneurial board, therefore, creates conditions that stimulate innovation and entrepreneurial activity. The first step involves setting up, within their own board meetings, a time to discuss innovation and new and future items. This practice is not only the specific vehicle through which the board introduces new ideas, but it also serves as a model for the agency overall. People will think that, if the board is doing it, it must be okay.

The second step is to set innovation as an evaluative dimension for the executive director or president, for staff, for board meetings, and for decisions. We discussed the mechanisms of this evaluation in Chapter 6 and do not need to repeat them here. Nonetheless, the executive or president will know when he or she is first hired that the board expects innovation and that it will be an ongoing element in his or her performance review. Simply doing the job the same old way will not be sufficient in this board's review process. New items, innovative items, and new approaches will have to be part of the review.

The third step is to develop a tolerance for failure. Innovations will not always succeed. Indeed, if they did, they probably would not be sufficiently innovative. Some ideas will not pan out. New therapeutic techniques will prove to be not as useful as some of the old ones. Opening a new field office might end up being a bad idea. The important thing is the fundamental entrepreneurial idea that success is built upon and draws its lessons from failure.

Comic actor John Cleese, best known as a member of the British comedy troupe, Monty Python, and for his roles in such films as *A Fish Called Wanda,* also has a company that produces management training films. Cleese says that if you don't risk failure or making mistakes, "you can't do, say anything useful" [1988]. He also points out that "a positive attitude towards mistakes [failure] will allow them to be corrected rapidly when they occur." Directors should adopt this attitude, both for themselves and for their organizations. Without the tolerance of mistakes, innovation will not develop.

The fourth step is to have policies that make exploration possible. We have already mentioned two: expectations of the executive at review time and setting aside some financial resources to allow experimentation. Many human service organizations budget themselves right up to 100% of their allocation. Funding for innovation has to come from surprise sources or occasional extra income that may happen to arrive, or from money freed up because of an early retirement or other personnel shift. If this is the fundamental approach to innovation—and it tends to be in organizations with conservative or traditional boards—then very little innovation will occur, because people cannot get the few bucks needed to attend a meeting to discuss a new idea with someone who is already doing it. Hence, the burden and costs of innovative land solely on the employee.

How much should be set aside for innovation? A good guideline is approximately 15% of an organization's budget. This may seem an astronomical sum. But consider C. Northcote Parkinson's idea that "work expands to fill the time in which you have to do it" [1957]. Allocations expand to fund the people on whom you have to spend it. It is a truism known to finance committees and others who deal with budgets that there is never enough money to do the things that any organization wants to do. Budgeting is a process of choice. Even if an agency's budget were doubled—and there have been cases where this has happened through a grant or some other activity—everyone would still be terribly short of resources. There is no end point where there will be enough left over to apply to innovation. Rather, boards must budget innovative activity as an ongoing, regular item and adjust other allocations around it. The important thing is to start budgeting some amount for innovation and development. For the board that does not have any innovation funding established, a three- to five-year plan involving a small percentage allocation each year is a good way to start.

This change in allocation might result in decreased services, but not necessarily. The reason has to do with economy and time. After an agency has been functioning for a while, its employees are generally able to do the same amount of work in less time (although not necessarily for less money, since the time for which they are paid as opposed to the time for which they work remains the same). Overall, organizations tend to do one of two things with this extra time. First, they might invest it in an organizational elaboration—more management, more committee meetings, and so on. They do the same "work" for more money.

Alternatively, organizations could devote some of the extra time to program elaboration—doing more of what they are already doing. They may undertake a few more clients or a few more programs. This kind of internal reallocation of organizational resources does not typically come to the attention of the board, but it represents an important allocative possibility. Instead of seeing more clients in the same way, perhaps they agency might try an innovative program. Hopefully, the expectation of innovation, signaled by adding innovation as a review element for the executive, will filter down to all of an agency's employees. Everyone might be expected to innovate within her or his realm.

The entrepreneurial board, therefore, tries to create a culture of innovation and implementation, constantly at the cutting edge of programs, services, and organizational forms. We all know organizations like this in our own communities. There is no reason why your organization cannot be one as well.

The 5-C Theory of Entrepreneurship

If entrepreneurial orientation is the more desirable orientation among those who are available for board service, is there any perspective or point of view that might help boards achieve this orientation? Yes. This theory [Tropman 1998] outlines five areas for directors to consider with respect to their own board and agency organization.

The 5 Cs of this theory are *characteristics, competencies, conditions, context,* and *change.* To be on the cutting edge of innovation and implementation, the organization's perspective must involve development in each area. Periodically, the board may wish to bring all members of the agency together in a 5-C conference to look at the interrelationship among the 5 Cs within the agency at a particular point and time. We discuss the 5-C conference in more detail below and again in Chapter 8.

The idea behind the 5-C theory is simple: New ideas and their development and implementation require an agency with people who possess certain *characteristics* and *competencies.* They also require that the agency have *conditions* that are stimulating and responsive to new ideas, and that these new ideas respond to the relevant *context* or environment. Thus, both individual elements and organizational and societal elements are involved. These elements are, of course, in a state of *change.* People and organizations are constantly changing and should be encouraged to change. As a final step, the articulation of these elements is crucial.

Historically speaking, entrepreneurship is not only identified with small business and profit-making enterprises, but with individuals as well. People frequently talk about the "natural" entrepreneur just as they speak of the "natural" leader or athlete, but this is too limiting. The "natural entrepreneur" concept invokes a passive rather than an active response to the development of a new idea, just as the concepts of a natural leader or a natural athlete invoke passive orientation toward leadership or athletics.

Another limitation is that such a view wrongly emphasizes the individual as the sole repository of whatever is needed for new developments and innovative programs. No matter how imaginative or innovative a particular new therapy or problem-solving technique may be, if the social agency is unwilling to try it and instead rejects it, then nothing more is likely to come from the innovation. Hence, there has to be a receptive climate, or condition, for the new idea as well. Finally, the new idea has to articulate (in the sense of both reflecting and leading) with the relevant context. A fantastic product with no market isn't going anywhere. An underserved service niche with no service available isn't going anywhere either. Hence, continual interaction is necessary.

This more elaborate perspective suggests that new ideas require individuals in the agency who have certain characteristics. Among these characteristics are tolerance for ambiguity, willingness to take risks, curiosity, a desire to be where the action is, and creativity. Periodically, boards of directors may wish to see whether people with these characteristics are present in their organizations and whether some directors, as board members, themselves have these characteristics. It will certainly help the innovative process.

But having characteristics is not enough, just as being creative and thinking up new ideas is never enough. One needs to be able, at various times, to have the intellectual and interpersonal skills (which we cover in Chapter 12 in a discussion of the role of the chair) through which these ideas can be taken a step further. Intellectual skills involve idea management, conceptualization, and synthesis. Once the germ of an idea has sprouted, it must be tended, cared for, looked after, and combined with other ideas. This aspect of competency requires intellectual skills. Similarly, interpersonal competencies are also necessary. A new idea will not sell itself; rather, opposition has to be persuaded. Organizational time and resources are well spent by attending to this particular new idea. Opposition, which always occurs in the realm of new ideas, must be diffused somewhat so that the new idea can be tried.

What is needed is an entrepreneurial team. After all, those who think up new ideas may not be the best at elaborating their details. Similarly, those who are good at detailed elaboration may not have the kind of creativity and fresh perspective that would generate a new idea in the first place. And those who have the interpersonal skills that can sell and persuade may not be the best at either thinking up or manipulating new ideas. An entrepreneurial team involves different individuals with different competencies and characteristics.

The organizational conditions must also be hospitable to innovation. Organizational conditions refer to a social agency's structure and culture. We have already mentioned the structural points: Is there a resource fund available? Is innovation an ongoing and expected part of the organization's activity? Is there space for innovation activities to take place? These structural features provide a supportive environment for the new idea or new program. Just as important, however, is the agency subculture with respect to innovation. Is performing some of the agency's activities in new and different ways prized, rewarded, featured, and showcased? Does the message of innovation get into the infrastructure of the organization as well as into the more formal aspects? Boards of directors must assure themselves that agency subculture and structure will support innovation.

Finally, boards must be attuned to context—the environment and the changes within that environment—as a potential source for opportunities and as a potential pressure for change. Too many organizations experience the "boiled-frog phenomenon." In this somewhat gruesome metaphor, Tichy and Devanna [1990] explain that if one places a frog in a petri dish full of water, and then slowly heats the water over a Bunsen burner, the frog will eventually boil to death. They explain that the barely noticeable difference in the frog's environment is never enough to cause the frog to jump out. Environmental changes are often like those tiny changes in the water in which the frog sits—small, not terribly noticeable, and not so drastic as to prompt action by common consent. Rather, every day and every year, things are just a little bit different. After several years, the agency may find itself unfunded. The board must respond to changes, therefore, by stimulating conditions, developing competencies, and encouraging characteristics that allow for innovation. But directors should do even more then that. Rather than waiting until change occurs and then responding to it, the entrepreneurial board seeks to test as yet undeveloped niches in the service needs of the community. By the time an environment or community can articulate its needs, it may already be too late.

Indeed, sometimes the environment does not know its needs. Post-it® notes are a good example. Society got along for years without those little sticky papers. If anyone had asked, "Do we need little sticky papers?" the answer surely would have been, "Of course not. We have paper clips and staples. Don't be silly." Yet Post-it® notes have become an almost indispensable feature of offices worldwide. The niche was there, the product met it, but until 3M translated that experimental idea into a marketable item, the need was unrecognized. Social agencies and their directors can take a lesson from this example.

The 5-C perspective helps directors of human service agencies to be aware of the elements that help them take a more entrepreneurially proactive role. Unfortunately, however, just being aware is not enough. Directors have to take specific and positive steps. Boards need a 5-C conference—an annual planning conference organized around the 5-C concept. The board asks different elements of the agency to assess agency characteristics, competencies, conditions, contexts, and changes. Then, the board and agency staff come together to talk about the mix among the agency's 5 Cs.

Results of course, cannot be foreordained. It may turn out that the agency has a wonderful mix—it has the competencies and characteristics necessary for the context in which it is operat-ing and the changes it is facing, and it has a supportive set of conditions. On the other hand, the context may have changed, new competencies may be needed, adjustments and conditions may be required, and new characteristics may be necessary. Holding regularly scheduled 5-C conferences permits continuous, ongoing focus on each of the 5 Cs, allowing the agency to develop sufficient articulation among them to remain at the cutting edge of human service delivery. The next chapter, on strategic change, provides some specific guidelines.

Playing All Four Roles

Although we can categorize boards as one of the four types—conservative, traditional, entrepreneurial, and overboard—consider that a board might fall into any one of these categories at any given time. Sometimes, a traditional posture is indeed appropriate; even a conservative posture may make sense under certain circumstances. Entrepreneurial orientations are appropriate in other instances, and, on occasion, even some overboard activity might be just what is needed. Boards will typically find themselves playing all four roles. The important point to keep in mind is to avoid becoming trapped in one or category or another.

Focusing on the 5-C theory of entrepreneurship for boards can help. That focus involves attention to the characteristics of those who work for the organization, the competencies they possess, the conditions that the organization sets up for itself, and the context in which the organization operates. Finally, the board needs to stimulate controlled change—through innovation, refurbishment, and strategic redesign, among other initiatives. Each of these requires constant scrutiny and oversight by the directors. An annual assessment of the interrelationship among these elements—the 5-C conference—can keep the agency current and even ahead of the game.

Exercise 6

Which board style best describes your board: conservative, traditional, entrepreneurial, or overboard?

Considering that all boards may exhibit some aspects of each style, what percentage of each type best applies to your board?

Conservative	_____
Traditional	_____
Entrepreneurial	_____
Overboard	_____
Total	100%

Could your board use a 5-C conference to become more entrepreneurial? How?

Chapter 8

Introducing Strategic Change

Individuals involved in board work are often struck with the permanence, if not intransigence, of board habits, board behaviors, and board culture. Understanding good board behavior is of limited use without the ability to introduce change into the board system. Obviously, many changes should be targeted to particular boards. Some general considerations are helpful, too.

The Benefits of Strategic Change

Many benefits accrue to the self-improving board, including a greater sense of board community, higher-quality decisions, and more involvement with community and staff. Directors often ask, "Why do we need to change?" There are many reasons [see Myers, Ufford, & McGill 1988].

A broader organizational picture. Most organizations, and especially boards, are only marginally aware of what their organizations are actually doing, when viewed as a whole. An overall assessment and strategic initiative allows a more global and a more in-depth picture of the kinds of activities an organization is undertaking and the costs and benefits of these activities.

A focus on facts. Many organizations are full of what Robert D. Vinter of the University of Michigan calls "lore": assertive statements about what the organization is or is not doing, has or has not done in the past, will or will not do in the future, and could or could not accomplish under a range of conditions. Such discussions, infrequently, are based on a common foundation of facts. A strategic initiative process should develop a focus on facts.

Shared identification of problems. A process of strategic change focuses on a shared perception of problems among stakeholders. Such sharing comes from interaction rather than assertion, from consensus rather than command, and requires time and effort to develop the common points of view that lead to sharing.

Identification of additional resources. Strategic change not only points to problems to be solved but frequently uncovers new resources with which those problems can be addressed.

Alternative solutions. The shared examination of problems and a focus on facts, combined with the broader organizational picture, allows the board to develop alternatives for every particular problem. Indeed, the options memo technique, discussed in Chapter 16, is a precise way of accomplishing this objective.

Team building. The common focus on board problems leads to a sense of team rather than competing camps within the organization. Frequently, too, a sense of excitement develops as old barriers to communication fall away.

Transferability. The process of strategic development within a board can be, and often is, applied to other areas in which directors and board affiliates (such as emeritus members or friends of the organization, for example) are involved. For this reason, strategic techniques are highly transferable.

Shift to the future. Many discussions of strategic plans, particularly at the board level, focus on defending the past. Individual identifications and egos become involved with programs that were doubtless appropriate for the time in which they were initiated but, with environmental changes, may now have become passé and, in some instances, even counterproductive. The ability to build on what is good right now, based on a generalized view of the environment, is key. The strategic process involves a revolution of expectations. These expectations reconfigure the interrelationships among community, agency, board, and task environment. They allow for the opening of new avenues of work and effort, and perhaps the closing of some old ones. But this repositioning is always essential. As the organization grows and changes, so too does the environment shift and develop. Thus, what was a good fit at one time, may be a relatively poorer fit now.

Requisites for Strategic Change

As directors begin to involve themselves in a process of strategic development, they face certain requisites and certain commitments that must be made from the beginning if the process is to succeed.

Frame of mind. Directors must approach their tasks with a different frame of mind. If they come into the room with a "show me" attitude, the process is almost doomed from the start. If, on the other hand, directors come in with a notion that "this time we are really going to make some changes and I, as a director, am going to be able to help in this process," the prognosis is much better.

Temporal commitment. Directors are extremely busy, and they often travel, so they are not always around as much as they thought they would be. Executives and others planning a strategic change should begin by being up front about the time required for the effort. Probably two or three days overall, including one day-long activity, will be necessary. Many might think this is too long, but it is modest when compared with the time lost through board rework, awful meetings, and similar horrors. If directors cannot make adequate time commitments from the beginning, the process starts with problems, and the board won't have the backup and investment necessary to accomplish the change.

Longer-range view. Many directors, especially under the press of time, will opt for quick fixes: "What's the problem? Let's do this, this, and this." The North American penchant for action supports the quick-fix solution. Yet, nearly every problem has causes or precipitating circumstances at multiple levels. One cause is the immediate precursor event; others might be more deeply rooted. Consider, for example, the voluntary organization whose United Way allocation was not received this year or was substantially reduced. The quick fix would be for the organization to replace those lost dollars with other funding and go about its business. If this were the organization's sole conclusion and action, however, it would be making a sorry mistake. Obvious reasons exist (though we may not know them clearly at first) as to why the local United Way did not make its allocation to the organization and what that might portend. The solution must involve more than just replacing the lost funding; the organization must fully understand and act upon the predisposing causes before it can respond effectively. The board has to set aside the immediate focus of finding a new funding source in favor of the longer-term view.

Facts and focus. In the initial stage, common and conventional preconceptions should be set aside. Everything that "everyone knows" should be viewed, at least at first, as suspect. One can always return, of course, to business as usual; but, since business as usual is what we are often trying to escape through such strategic initiatives, we should first agree to some kind of intellectual independence, an openness to new thinking, which can be a freeing, inspiriting, creative process.

Better ideas. Finally, the board needs to better recognize itself as a source of new ideas. All too often, we tip our hats in acknowledgment to groups, to the group process, and to strategic decision making, and then return to the old, individualistic, supposedly long-range approaches that have been so comfortable for us in the past. Whether they were truly long range, of course, is an open question.

How to Achieve Strategic Change

How do directors, executives, and agency staff go about achieving the benefits of strategic change? One answer is leadership. Leadership involves developing a vision of where the organization might be. Leadership may come from anywhere within the organization. A typical mistake assumes that leadership only comes from the agency's president, executive, or board chair. Fortunate is the organization that has leadership resources in each position. Often, however, leadership must come from other directors or from staff before the organization can undertake a strategic change.

Individuals who are interested in introducing strategic change into an agency must often wait for an event that precipitates a willingness to act. A driver education teacher once said, "An accident really focuses your attention on driving." All the injunctions about driving carefully really do not hit home until someone actually has been involved in an accident and experienced the trauma it can create. Hopefully, it is a small accident, and the benefits of learning far outweigh the inconveniences and difficulties.

A similar point applies to agencies and boards of directors. Frequently, a small leadership group within the organization sees the need for change. Despite their discussions with other directors, agency members, and selected community leaders, they may be unable to generate an interest in and momentum for strategic change until a cataclysmic event occurs. That event might be the sudden departure or resignation of an agency president or executive. It could involve severe criticism in the media about something that happened within the organization. Or it might be the agency's failure to secure an expected piece of funding. The list could go on. The point is that although organizational readiness for strategic change requires leadership, leadership alone is not always successful. Sometimes, difficult, troubling events must occur to create the kind of organizational concern necessary to move the process forward.

Once an organization is ready to change, how should it proceed? An on-site analysis is one approach [Myers, Ufford, & McGill 1988]. A consulting team arrives on site and orchestrates the process of strategic change. This process may be too costly or otherwise beyond the organization's reach, however.

The SWOT Analysis

As an alternative, the organization may wish to engage its own volunteers in a strategic change process using a technique known as a "SWOT analysis," followed by a "5-C conference." SWOT analyses are relatively common in the field of strategic planning. Had the agency contracted with an outside consultant, the consultant likely would have used this method.

A SWOT analysis involves examining the agency from four different perspectives: strengths, weaknesses, opportunities, and threats—hence the term *SWOT*. Teams of directors, staff, and other who might be interested, review the agency's position vis-à-vis these four variables, keeping in mind the injunctions mentioned earlier in this chapter. Usually, these four teams are coordinated through the office of the CEO, for such reasons as budget or management. Having a planner or consultant assist in the process may also be helpful; sometimes that person may become a resource as well.

One team reviews the organization's strengths. What are its strong points? What are the things for which it is known, today and in the past? How might these strengths be capitalized, extended, or converted to new purposes? The strength assessment group examines these and other related questions.

Paralleling an organization's strengths are its weaknesses. A "weakness team" thinks about the problems the organization is facing. What are the points of difficulty? The areas of low quality? The areas of trouble? The weakness team must take particular care to be honest, open, and direct. Every organization, like every person, has strengths and weaknesses. Organizations, like people, tend to overstate their strengths and minimize their weaknesses. Indeed, listening to many individuals in an organization describe themselves, one would think that the agency's weaknesses were either infinitesimal or nonexistent. Clearly, personal and organizational defense mechanisms are at work here, and powerfully so. To obtain a fair and honest picture of what is really troubling an organization, these defense mechanisms must be set aside.

A third team looks at opportunities in the environment. What opportunities might be available for this particular organization? Are they being exploited now, or could they be exploited in the future? Is the environment changing so as to make new opportunities likely? For example, colleges and universities well know that, following a "baby boom" comes a "baby bust," with fewer students in the college-age bracket.

Naturally, colleges and universities will seek to expand the proportion of college-age people who actually attend college. It is also possible, however, and even desirable, to redefine what "college age" means. Many universities are aggressively seeking older students—in their 30s, 40s, 50s, and even 60s—who have a yearning for an education that they were not able to complete at an earlier age, or who simply seek to expand their knowledge. One must first see the opportunity in the older student, however, before one can pursue it.

Finally, a fourth team assesses threats to the organization. What in the environment might harm the organization? Have government allocations become increasingly uncertain? Has a particular residential treatment center, run by an agency, had a string of difficulties that have drawn the attention of accrediting groups? Is there an ominous decline in the number of people who are interested in working for the agency at the current wage rates? These and other questions represent an analysis of the threats facing the agency. Threats may link with weaknesses; in fact, if an unfortunate confluence of threats and weaknesses occurs—if threats seem to come in areas of weakness—then the agency is in a perilous state.

There is no special formula for carrying out these analyses, although the large amount of material available on strategic planning suggest a variety of ways to approach it. The main point is to "just do it." Once the analysis is complete, agency members come together, often in a retreat format, to discuss the findings and to plot new directions. Presumably, new directions arise from a consideration of strengths and opportunities on the positive side and a scrutiny of threats and weaknesses on the negative side. The process seeks to neutralize threats and reduce the impact of weaknesses while augmenting strengths and seizing opportunities. This small exercise can really help an organization avoid trouble in the process of self-renewal.

The 5-C Conference

It is very difficult, however, and not really helpful, to undergo strategic planning every year. The process becomes tiresome and unproductive. The organization should therefore try to establish, on an annual basis, a 5-C retreat.

The 5 Cs, as outlined in Chapter 7, are the characteristics and competencies of people; conditions of the organization; context, or the environment; and change. The board will probably find it most helpful to conduct a 5-C assay annually. A 5-C assay is similar to a SWOT analysis, but not as complex. It simply involves small groups of people—again, coordinated by the CEO's office—looking at the characteristics of individuals within, and served by, the agency, and those who serve on the board; the competencies of the staff and the directors; the conditions, structure, and culture of the organization; the contexts within which the organization operates; and the changes that are needed and that are under way. Findings are reported at an annual 5-C retreat, where the board and agency members discuss the fit between and among characteristics, competencies, conditions, contexts, and change. The 5-C retreat allows an ongoing, less painful adjustment to shifts in the environment, in the mix of personal characteristics, in competencies or the need for certain competencies, and in changes in organizational conditions and contexts. The 5-C conference is less dramatic and volcanic than a SWOT analysis and, because it is done yearly, less threatening. Adjustments required as a result of the 5-C review are smaller.

The annual 5-C retreat does not circumvent the need for a SWOT analysis. Indeed, one might want to use a SWOT analysis as a basis for the five- to seven-year organizational renewal requirement, which we discussed in Chapter 5. If the environment is turbulent, however, the intervals between strategic assessments should be shortened! The

5-C review, however, does allow for an ongoing, regularized attempt to look at the members of the agency and the tasks and problems the organization faces, and to make adjustments as necessary.

Getting Ready for Strategic Planning

As boards begin strategic planning, it is imperative that they think through what the process requires. The first step is to review the perspectives and requisites of strategic blending so that directors have a common understanding of the energies that will be required and a common agreement to set aside presuppositions, predefinitions, and simple solutions, and to adopt a readiness to explore new opportunities. This readiness must come before all else. The Professional Unit System and the Index of Dissimilarity—which we discuss in Chapter 13—are useful techniques for the strategic planning process. Without that original readiness, however, the tools one uses will not make much difference—progress will not occur.

Exercise 7

Does your board or agency have a strategic plan? How old is it? Does anyone use it?

Has the structure of the board been aligned with the strategic plan?

Plan a SWOT analysis for your board.

Part III

How to Do It: Board Organization, Development, and Evaluation

"On second thought, <u>don't</u> correct me if I'm wrong."

How to Do It: Board Organization, Development, and Evaluation

Overview

Knowing what to do is one thing. Being able to do it is something else. Those with whom we talked emphasized five requisite elements necessary for boards to function properly:

- Boards have to be organized properly and have the right committees.
- They must attest to the balances between executive and board, and between internally and externally focused activities.
- Boards must train themselves so that they improve over time.
- Directors must know how to carry out their positions.
- Finally, they have to evaluate themselves, their decisions, and their processes.

Chapter 9

Proper Board Organization

The board's functions are many and varied. Typically, an entire board cannot accomplish all of its functions as a "committee of the whole," so most boards break up into committees and subcommittees to address the different tasks.

Board consultants suggest—and our own investigations confirm—that approximately half of a board's time is wasted in unnecessary agenda items—for example, items for which there is insufficient information to allow the board to act. Board organization that can process items and bring options to the full board for consideration, therefore, is one of the most important elements of quality decision making. Without an appropriate committee structure, it is very difficult for the board to properly carry out its decision-making and oversight role.

In general, the makeup of most board committees should include at least one director from the board itself, but no more than three. Other committee members come from the visiting committee, leadership circle, or advisory board, as we discussed in Chapter 3.

Committees and Subcommittees

The board should not approach its issues casually or in an offhand manner, but rather with sustained thought. Boards operate much better when working from the recommendations of committees. With rare exceptions, therefore, the

board should assign upcoming tasks to committees, request-
ing that they study their assigned matters with appropriate
staff, other members of the organization, and the community
at large to develop proposals for action with alternative considerations, and present their recommendations to the board.
Without having to both acquire relevant information and
make decisions, the board can deal with issues much more
effectively and efficiently.

Key committees fall into three groups: operating, strategic, and ad hoc.

Operating Committees

There are commonly seven key operating committees with
important ongoing functions for most organizations. Their
functions may be combined, however, within a smaller
number of committees. Although, in many ways, the strategic committees may be more important—for it is within the
strategic committees that the organization's programmatic
elements find expression—the operating committees are
essential to run the organization.

- **The executive committee** comprises the board president, its officers, the executive director, and the
  chairs from the board's other committee. The executive committee can usually take action in emer-
  gency situations when the full board cannot meet,
  and it often sorts out those activities and proposals that need board approval. The executive
  committee coordinates the work of the other committees and takes overall responsibility for the
  operation of the board itself.

- **The budget and finance committee** generates the
  organizational budget and handles financial oversight, reviewing financial trajectories monthly, at

least, and sometimes weekly. It works with the organization's chief budget or financial officer in preparing budgets, making proposals for new expenditures, and other such fiscal matters. The budget and finance committee should involve people from the financial community to facilitate access to banks and other local sources of financing when necessary, but this committee should involve others as well! The budget and finance committee reports to the board on both overall budgetary strategy and specific budget proposals.

- **The financial resource development committee** develops financial resources for the organization. Its activities may involve seeking public contributions, planning fundraising events, securing grants, or developing contributions of property. All directors should have the opportunity to serve on this committee at some point in their tenure on the board. Because raising resources is such a difficult task, people can tire of it quickly and burn out. Regularly rotating directors on and off this committee can help keep its members fresh and its work invigorated. Too, actually raising the funds that one spends introduces a note of realism into the allocations process.

- **The human resource development committee** oversees the organization's human resources. Traditionally, this body has been called the "personnel" committee, but that is too narrow a construct. The committee does, of course, develop the personnel policies for the organization, but its role is larger. It helps provide the resources necessary for the staff and board to do their jobs, through development and training. (With board activities, it works with the recruitment and training committee.) It stays in touch with staff and their concerns on the one hand, as well with as the broader human resources community on the other. Its purview can involve such issues as compensation, holidays, and employee burn out. The personnel committee also typically handles grievances and the identification, interviewing, and review of top agency staff.

- **The public relations committee** enhances and improves the agency's image with the general public. It prepares annual reports, newsletters, press releases, and other pieces of public information and seeks favorable publicity about the agency. Sometimes the board may merge public relations and community relations into one committee, but the function of public relations tends to be focused more on media.

- **The community relations committee** focuses on the personal aspects of community involvement—for example, organizing tours of the agency, providing speakers for public functions, and interpreting the agency's mission and role to key people in the community. Whereas the public relations committee tends to concentrate on the media, the community relations committee focuses on people. Its role often relates to government, and this committee frequently cultivates relationships with political figures at the local, state, and national levels and seeks to develop political clout for the organization.

- **The board recruitment and training committee**
  seeks to interest previously uninvolved individuals in the organization, its mission, and role. The
  recruitment and training committee may maintain
  a list of potential board members—"good" people
  who might be interested in serving on the board.
  In recruitment, the committee meets with individuals, interprets the kind of job the agency is doing,
  and promotes that person's involvement with the
  organization. The nominating function, which
  usually occurs annually to develop a slate of
  officers for the board, also may be the responsibility of this committee. But, whereas the nominating function moves people who have already
  participated in the organization (from the outer
  circle of the advisory or visiting committee) into
  full directorship and into officers' positions on the
  board, the role of recruitment is to secure people
  from outside the organization and bring them
  into this outer circle.

  In training, this committee is responsible for
  preparing a board members' manual (see Chapter
  11), conducting annual training sessions for the
  entire board, and providing additional training for
  individual directors if they so desire. In this task,
  it works with the human resources development
  committee.

Strategic Committees

These committees are driven by the mission but largely by
the strategic plan. That document identifies targets of
emphasis—usually three or four things that constitute the

organization's core activities. Each of these items should have its own committee for oversight and encouragement.

Strategic committees promote the structure and purpose for the mission and role of the agency itself. Agencies usually have somewhat general missions and roles that need concrete manifestations in the form of specific programs. Some activities need to be undertaken, and others stopped. All activities need monitoring and evaluation. A strategic committee often comprises professionals in the area of concern and lay people or volunteers interested in making program recommendations to the board. Strategic committees generally work closely (perhaps most closely) with staff.

Ad Hoc Committees

The board can form ad hoc committees for specific events or tasks. These committees are helpful because they are not permanent and can operate for the short term.

Too Many Committees?

Boards can have too many committees. Some committee functions can be combined. The point is to make the work of the board more efficient and effective. As we shall see in Chapters 15–17 on board meetings, each committees does not report at each meeting; a committee only reports when an issue requires discussion or a decision. Hence, the board avoids meeting clutter.

Board organization can be one of the most effective ways to position the board to carry out its functions. Organizations should pay careful attention to the way in which they set up their boards and the changes their individual board structures require.

Exercise 8
Board Organization

Does your board have a satisfactory structure?

Is it about the right size?

Does it have appropriate committees?

Does it have both standing and ad hoc committees?

Considering some of the ideas in this chapter, how could your board's structure be improved?

Chapter 10

Balancing Inward and Outward Focus

Boards play a range of internal and external roles in the process of carrying out their missions. Directors must understand the various roles and the issues surrounding them.

Individual directors and the board itself are responsible for acting appropriately within the context of their roles. We have discussed the individual requisites of those roles, particularly as they regard legal responsibilities and the avoidance of self-aggrandizement and self-profit. More importantly, we have stressed the positive aspects of one's personal role—acting as a trustee of civic purpose and taking a proactive, accomplishment-oriented posture. More detailed discussions of the roles of the board chair, director, executive director, and staff member can help flesh out these suggestions.

Society in the late 1990s, however, is taking an increasingly closer look at the ethical behavior of civil and civic servants. Directors are more aware that simply wanting to "do good" is not good enough. In many ways, society holds those in the voluntary sector to higher standards than those elsewhere.

The Role of the Board

The way in which the board performs and presents its role—to itself and to the community—is very important. Both the board and its individual directors have certain functions to perform if the organization is to achieve its overall purpose. The board needs a structure so it can perform its internal and external functions. The directors need to work toward both board performance and appropriateness.

Distinguishing between decision making (generally an internal function) and advice giving (generally an external function) is especially important. Overall, boards' responsibilities typically involve three internal and four external functions.

Internal Functions

Policy decisions typically relate to the board as a whole and involve the board's formal legal authority as specified under the organization's articles of incorporation and state statute. Decisions made under this function are typically referred to as policy decisions, although other types of decisions may have policy impact as well. Crucial to this function are adequate information, adequate time for review, adequate feedback from appropriate parties, and reasonably prompt action consistent with the available information.

Directors should avoid "decisional prematurity" and "decisional postmaturity." Prematurity occurs when an item comes to a policy-deciding meeting without adequate information. Typically, the board spends a great deal of time on such issues, then postpones a decision. Decisional prematurity is one of the most significant causes of decisional postmaturity. Too often, a decision delayed is a decision denied. It is legitimate for a director to charge a board with undue delay. The question of what is undue, however, is a difficult one, and it generally cannot be solved. Although there is no issue for which more information cannot be garnered and on which additional perspectives would not be useful, external constraints, such as grant deadlines, fiscal year deadlines, and so on, often make the very best informed decision useless if it comes too late. Within the policy-deciding function, therefore, boards must balance information and decisional needs and pressures.

Policy oversight is typically accomplished through the committee structure. This function involves generating policy and reviewing components, as well as assessment and program audits. Policy oversight occurs once the board makes a formal decision. Oversight does not occur until the decision is made. Within the concept of policy oversight, however, is a certain amount of policy proactivity—the anticipation of upcoming events and the proposed adjustment of existing policies to take those new events into account. Members of policy oversight groups must be clear about the scope and extent of the particular policies they are monitoring, and they should neither overextend their role to encompass tangential areas nor ignore or minimize the responsibilities that they do have.

Policy administration. Sometimes, given unique situations, the board may establish a policy-administering committee. For example, in an agency crisis, the board may delegate power to a small group—along with appropriate financial resources, staff, and logistical support—to immediately handle, with the executive, the particular situation. Most typically, fast-breaking situations require such a task force or ad hoc group. The task force dissolves when the situation is resolved.

Over the course of a year, a board will very typically perform all of these functions, plus the following external functions. The board must be sensitive to the different issues it will encounter in each of these areas.

External Functions

Boards of human service agencies play a series of four external roles that are quite different from their internal roles. As agencies move into the interorganizational environment, they no longer have the imperative control given them by their charters and articles of incorporation. Rather, they move from a position based on authority to one based on cooperation, which involves networking and coalition building. In this environment, boards may play four external roles: policy sharing, policy advising, policy coordination, and policy implementation. Sometimes, boards may create other community committees that play these roles too.

Policy sharing. In this role, the board agrees to cooperate with other similar agencies so they may become acquainted with each other's ongoing programs. Such sharing does not imply any adjustment in either's programs, nor that any particular program is right or wrong, or appropriate or inappropriate. It simply reflects an agreement to get together and "show and tell" agency programs. This activity reflects a cooperative posture only.

Policy advising. Sometimes, a board may be asked for a collective opinion on a matter of community concern. The mayor, for example, may call and ask what the agency thinks about an issue. Simply letting the executive write a quick recommendation is not sufficient. Rather, the directors must discuss matter and prepare language that reflects the board's perspective. The recommendation must be approved by the board and entered into the minutes. Although the board is actually making a decision in this policy advisory process, the decision is only advice.

Policy coordination. Policy sharing sometimes leads to policy coordination. The board might be asked to approve a policy to share responsibility for a program with other agencies. For example, one agency might suggest to another, "We'll handle young children, and you handle older kids," or "We'll handle boys, and you handle girls." This kind of coordination requires agreement from the board. Organizational staff need to be involved as well. Agency or organizational coordination requires joint planning and agreement.

Policy implementation. Within the interorganizational system, the board of directors might become part of a team asked to implement a particular community-wide decision. Again, such an arrangement calls for delegated functions and those that require constant board oversight and approval. A director from an agency board who joins a community-wide group to coordinate and implement a community program does not carry any kind of board approval unless his or her board has specifically given such approval.

These are important functions for boards to play, and we strongly encourage boards to participate in policy sharing, policy coordination, and policy implementation at the community level. In such situations, however, the board might create a special committee or task force to handle the organization's relationship with the constellation of other organizations that are seeking to accomplish a larger social task.

Balancing Focus

Certainly, boards can play many other roles. These seven, however, divided between internal and external focus, are the most common and suggest some of the different dynamics that boards can expect to encounter.

Boards tend to be more inwardly focused, playing roles as corporate citizens in the collective community less and less frequently. Striking a balance between the inward and outward focuses is appropriate, but a balance dictates that boards spend some time in coordinating, implementing, sharing, and advisory roles. Boards should pay more attention to the external roles than they have historically—particularly in the human service community. Decision-making boards often find it difficult to play these external roles because they relinquish the authority they have with internal matters. This shift from an authoritative to a cooperative posture can be a challenge for a board, but one that the board must carry out.

Exercise 9

Consider the seven board policy roles:

Internal	**External**
Decision	Sharing
Oversight	Advising
Administration	Coordination
	Implementation

Has your board played all of these roles?

Which roles does it play best?

Which does it play worst?

Does the board adjust its behavior when its roles shift?

Chapter 11

The Board as
Trainer and Developer

Boards have a responsibility for training new and current directors. Several cases illustrate why this is necessary. For example, during the community development efforts in the United States in the 1960s, well-intentioned people aimed for the "maximum feasible participation" of low-income people. As Senator Daniel Patrick Moynihan (D-NY) [1969] put it, what came out was, mostly, "maximum feasible misunderstanding."

During that time, many people who lacked board experience were brought onto the governing bodies of nonprofit charitable organizations. Rarely did they receive any kind of orientation, yet they were often blamed for their own "failures." Other examples from both the profit and nonprofit sectors abound. We all know stories of boards acting too late or with too little energy, and the crises that often follow for those organizations.

The bad news is that boards have been insufficiently vigorous in the past. The good news is that they are waking up. The problem that "waking up" creates further emphasizes the need to provide directors with training in boardship. Orientation is an absolute necessity for new directors; ongoing training is even more so for all directors.

The Board Manual

The first step in any training and development is to have the books. In this case, the book is a board manual. Every organized board should develop a manual for its directors.

The board manual should open with a statement of the organization's mission, its purpose, and its *raison d'être*—its reason for existing—followed by a brief history of the organization. The manual should then detail the organization's legal responsibilities, referring the reader to the articles of incorporation in an appendix.

Following these opening sections, the manual should include a statement on the expected responsibilities of directorship, outlining the role of the typical director. This is a job description for the director, one that will be used for evaluation later on.

The next section, which can be replaced regularly, should deal with the organization's current strategic plan and operating structure. Detail committees and their functions, as well as advisory committees and any important links; provide names, addresses, and telephone numbers of current and past directors; and describe plans for training program for directors, retreat dates, and meeting schedules—all of the specific information that directors might need. Include the names and addresses of staff on a separate sheet that can be updated as necessary.

Another section should contain a compilation of annual reports. This gives each director an opportunity to see what the agency has done over time and to consider what it is likely to do in the future. Future plans can also be listed here. In addition, a single summary sheet can give historical demographic facts about the agency, such as its annual budget or per capita expenditures on children.

Sample Table of Contents for a Board of Directors Manual

Directors' Manual
The Children's Center
Table of Contents

  I. Mission and Purpose of the Organization

     A. History

     B. Philosophy

 II. Legal Responsibilities

     A. In general, for all board members

     B. In particular, for this particular board

III. Responsibilities and Duties of Board Membership

IV. Current Operating Structure

     A. Strategic plan

     B. Organizational plan

     C. Current and past directors, names and addresses

     D. Committees

     E. Financial information

     F. Program plans, schedules

  V. Annual Reports

 VI. Future Plans

VII. Appendix: Articles of Incorporation

Finally, include any pertinent reading material the board feels is essential to the director. These materials can include helpful copies of current articles, as well as a relevant bibliography if that's appropriate.

This is only a skeletal suggestion for a board manual. Some manuals are simple and direct; others are more complicated and intricate. What is vital is that the board itself develop its own manual. A suggested table of contents for a board directors' manual appears on page 111.

Board Training

One of the most important board training activities is the training session for new director. If the board has used the two-tier process we described in Chapter 3—involving prospective directors in the organization by first inviting their service on a visiting committee, advisory board, or leadership circle—the new director will not begin from zero. This is too often the case, and it frequently takes six months to a year for the new director to become a useful participating member. In either case, whether the new director has participated in ancillary groups or is inexperienced, an orientation process should occur. It need not be long, but it should include two basic aspects.

The first deals with the organization's substantive elements—its purpose, mission, and commitment. New directors need to know what they are getting into before they can make substantial contributions. The second part of this training should deal with the principles of good group decision making. This section of the training program can be linked to training for other individuals on the board—indeed, it is very good if this is the case. Mutual education involving discussion, participation, and the acquisition of new knowledge is a very good way to establish the bonding between new directors and veterans that makes effective and efficient decision making possible.

Board Development

Although too few boards have proper training procedures for directors, even fewer have policies regarding the development of the board and individual directors. What's the difference? Board training is specific and focuses directly on the specific missions of the organization in question. Board and director development focuses on the education of the board and the director, toward a more general set of skills and competencies. The rationale for board development is the same that supports professional and staff development anywhere. Staff need training, of course, in the specifics of the agency, but they also need to experience development— the general education that comes from attending conferences and participating in seminars. That same expectation and benefit is due directors.

The board should provide for and establish an expectation of one development activity per director per year. Such an activity can be individual—a particular director going to a conference of interest to him or her—or it can be a collective effort, in which the board brings in someone to provide some educational component for the entire group. The important feature here is that directors have opportunities to grow during their tenure on the board.

Networking

Some aspects of director training are costly and too difficult for one agency to conduct alone. Directors may wish to network with other organizations and create training and development opportunities in cooperation with other agencies—a "Saturday Seminar," for example. Or, the board may wish to work with a key community resource agency, like the United Way, to sponsor and develop such sessions.

A Task Ignored

The development of directors is one of the very deficient areas in contemporary nonprofit boards. Investment in director development pays large dividends.

Exercise 10

Review your board's training and development activities.

Are they adequate?

If not, why not?

Can you think of ways to improve them?

Chapter 12

Board Positions

Much of this book so far has focused on the more formal or mechanical elements in directing and governing nonprofit organizations. Personal dynamics are involved as well, however. What does one actually do as the board chair or as a director on the board of a nonprofit organization? What specific activities and expectations do these roles involve? These questions deserve some attention, not only because they relate centrally to the performance of nonprofit directors, but also because directors often find themselves in board positions before they fully understand what the roles entail.

Board performance should be both efficient and effective. Efficiency refers to the economical use of time. If, through preparation, one can reduce the amount of time one spends on an activity, so much the better. The other goal is effectiveness—spending time on the right topics. Successful performance of one's role stresses both of these elements as interdependent and interlinked.

The Chair

The role of the board chair is one of the most complex in the nonprofit field. So many expectations and hopes rest with the chair—from being the custodian of the organization's tradition, to running efficient meetings, to providing leadership for new directions. Finding and developing committee chairs is a difficult enough task for the executive director (in consultation with the nominating committee, of course). Finding and developing a good board chair is even more difficult.

Often, the experience of chairing the board is a trying one for the incumbent as well as for the other directors, and sometimes for the whole agency. Problems frequently occur because the new chair does not fully understand the roles of leadership and organizational development that devolve upon the chair and upon the board as a whole. Board chairs sometimes feel that, to do their jobs, they have to become deeply involved with their agencies' ongoing daily operations. They fail to realize that the leader's job focuses much more on creating expectations than on action—that doing more is not as important as expecting more. We sometimes attribute a chairperson's poor performance to his or her own personal characteristics. There is no question that some people are, for example, power hungry, abrasive, or indecisive. More likely, however, is that the chairperson's poor performance results from his or her unawareness of the kinds of roles the chair should play and the kinds of actions he or she should take—and the chair often receives little help in preparing for the role.

Preparation for the Chair's Role

There is much wisdom in avoiding a direct move into the role of chair before performing a subsidiary or related role within the organization. Often, people—particularly those who have performed a range of civic leadership functions—get tapped for organizational roles simply because of their personal prestige and status and the skills they demonstrated in those other roles. The appeals are often seductive: The recruiting agency flatters the ego of the potential chairperson while minimizing—and possibly not sharing at all—some of the problems and difficulties it might be experiencing.

Thus, a key guideline for anyone who is considering an offer to chair a nonprofit board—and a key requirement of any organization seeking to recruit a new chair—should be for that person to have at least one year's experience with the organization's board before assuming a formal leadership position. Many agencies have incorporated this piece of wisdom into their bylaws; they move people up the organizational hierarchy through a series of positions: second vice chair, then first vice chair, leading to the position of chair. Of course, although this is sensible for organizations that have candidates in abundance, many organizations would find this approach problematic since they do not have enough people to fill these positions. The idea behind this policy is still a good one, however. Not only should individuals avoid taking formal leadership positions without prior experience, but organizations should avoid proposing such appointments. The work of the nominating committee, mentioned in Chapter 3 as an important activity, should help prevent some of these difficulties.

This is the usual route. Sometimes, however, an organization may deliberately bring in a new chair who is not acquainted with the agency, often to shake things up. That person must receive special orientation.

Preacceptance Activities

Let's assume that one is contemplating the chair's position because of personal interest, an invitation from the board, or a combination of the two. What tasks should one accomplish before assuming the role?

The statesperson perspective. The person moving into the role of the chair must assume the perspective of a statesman—a "statesperson," to be gender neutral—rather than of a partisan. The typical director may have specific interests, programs, and ideas that he or she wishes to pursue, promoting them vigorously in board meetings. This desire is fine—indeed, directors should introduce and fight for ideas. The board chair, however, must set aside the perspective of promoting her or his personal agenda. ("Now that I'm the chair, I can push what I want.") Certainly, the chairperson will have ideas and will provide leadership for ideas. The hallmark of the chair's role, however, is much more the blending and orchestrating of others' ideas. The chair becomes a statesperson.

The situation is much like that of a first violinist who becomes conductor of the orchestra. Taking to heart the perspectives and problems of the entire orchestra, the new conductor must schedule musical compositions that reflect and showcase the range of talent present in the orchestra, not just the strings. Statesmanship is perhaps the most important of the preacceptance tasks, or "prework," that potential board chairs must undertake.

Assess the other directors. The second piece of prework is a detailed assessment of the other directors on the board. We often work with people in organizational settings without knowing much about them. The board chair has to understand the other directors' motivations: Why did they join the board? What do they hope to gain from involvement? What ideas, skills, and interests might they contribute? Answering these and other questions gives the new chair a better understanding of the people with whom he or she will be working. Even though the board chair may work with other directors over long periods of time, such an association does not means that the chair knows the interests and motivations of those individuals in any depth.

One way to explore the interests of other directors is to schedule short meetings with the others—a phone call or coffee. The chair can explore the interests and commitments of each director; this can provide lots of information that can inform committee assignments, special assignments, and other duties. This method may be time-consuming, but it's useful.

Conditions of appointment. The third piece of prework the chair-to-be should undertake is to negotiate any resources, special help, and particular undertakings of interest that are conditions of appointment. As with any job, there is a period of negotiation when one agrees to fill the position of board chair. Those negotiations are very difficult to recapture once one has accepted and is in office. Not all chairpersons may have such special demands, but one should explore one's own interests to see if any exist. A discussion with the other directors—"I'll be happy to be chair, but I would like the board to develop a strategic plan as a condition for my acceptance"—is perfectly legitimate. Of course, the chair-to-be may not get all of his or her wishes, but the chances are greater at the early negotiating window than after acceptance. Many a chair has sadly lamented, "Well, I assumed that when I took over the chair we would be doing...."

Self-assessment. Finally, the chair must do some self-assessment. The appointment of a chair is a signal to other directors, the executive director, and agency staff. The chairperson-to-be must understand how others may regard him or her, even if that reading is somewhat inaccurate. For example, if the new chair is an accountant or someone from the financial community, some may take the appointment as an indication of financial tightening and a focus on financial matters. If the new chair is from the human relations field, then some might assume that a human relations focus is coming. These assumptions may not be accurate, but they inform the behavior of others and, hence, must be taken into account.

If all of these elements can be satisfied, then the chair-to-be should feel free to undertake the responsibility. Going through these steps may seem problematic and time-consuming, but the problems that new board chairs have experienced over the years suggest that undertaking these steps can enhance success. Of course, we have to correct for realism. It's not likely that everyone can do all of these things. If there are too many prerequisites, no one will ever get to be chair. But these prework tasks are a good place to start.

After Acceptance

The chairperson has now assumed the formal chair position. After accepting the chair, what roles does the chair play? How, specifically, can the chair carry out his or her responsibilities as chair during the course of regular board meetings? Overall, the chair's responsibilities fall into three broad areas:

- **Operational responsibilities,** or working with the executive or president. These responsibilities deal with running the place.

- **Intellectual responsibilities,** or developing ideas. These aspects of the chair's roles involve generating, supporting, and managing ideas. Without leadership from the chair, new ideas are not likely to surface, and old ideas are not likely to receive careful review and rethinking, resulting in either premature or "postmature" decisions based on inadequate or "overadequate" information. Chairs have to help groups consider topics and reach decisions.

- **Interpersonal responsibilities,** or developing people. This involves the "people part"—enhancing participation, involving those who hang back, and dealing diplomatically with troublesome and difficult individuals.

Let's consider each in more detail.

Operational responsibilities

The board chair and the organization's executive director or president work hand in hand to provide a central leadership team. As part of the preparatory discussions, the chair-to-be should have an opportunity to consider a range of issues with the executive director so as to avoid any surprises on either side. The executive director is frequently involved in recruiting the chair because every executive director knows that the chair's leadership is crucial to the ultimate success of the organization in general and to the executive director's career in particular. The executive director and the chair should map out areas of agreement between them of both substance and process.

On the substantive side, the chair and executive director should agree in advance on the goals they want to emphasize and the strategic matters that will influence the overall direction of the organization in the coming year. This should not preclude other directors on the board raising issues or putting fresh items on the agenda; but, at the very least, the executive director and the chair should have some understanding of where they are going and what they would like to do. Difficulty or disagreement between the chair and the executive can bring the organization to a standstill.

On the procedural side, the chair and the executive director should agree on how they will carry out their respective positions and roles. Some chairs like to give executive directors a great deal of latitude; others want executives to keep them more directly informed. Typically, new chairs like to receive more information at first, a practice that often diminishes as the working relationship between the executive and the chair grows.

The executive and the chair should discuss differences in their styles frankly and honestly before the new chair takes office. What participation does the executive director want to have in meetings? How does the new chair feel about this level of participation? Does the new chair want the executive director to work toward any particular style? The two leaders should iron out these issues and others as fully as possible so that they each understand the other's wishes. Human relationships being what they are, disagreements will always arise, but such a prior discussion will help minimize the problems.

The chair should meet regularly with the executive or president to review agency matters, plan meetings, and think through issues. Little can substitute for these regular meetings. This means that the chair has at least three sets of regular meetings to attend—the meeting with the executive, the executive committee meeting, and the regular full board meeting.

Intellectual responsibilities

The chair has responsibilities for processing and developing ideas and for improving and refurbishing the general policies of the organization. The chair must undertake several activities in this regard.

Policy agenda. Every new chair should establish a policy agenda for the coming year. This policy agenda comes from the strategic plan, which, presumably, the organization has put together to cover the agency's direction for the next two or three years. If there is no strategic plan, one of the chair's earliest jobs is to get the organizational process under way and produce a strategic plan within a year or so.

Assuming a strategic plan does exist, however, the chair identifies key areas of policy work for the coming year. The board may have already chosen some items for its policy agenda, because the strategic plan may necessitate that some activities be undertaken within specified time frames. Or the plan may be more general than that, giving the new chair an opportunity to set some areas of his or her own interests as policy priorities—after discussion, of course, with other directors, the executive, and agency staff via the executive director.

Additionally, the board should undertake an annual policy review and refurbishment, as we discussed in Chapter 5. If controversy and conflict arise over a particular policy area, the policy review may occur sooner than once a year, of course. Agency conflict often results, however, in the absence of such a review. Policies become outdated, provide insufficient guidance, or become a source of crisis and difficulty for the agency. Revisitation and review can help avoid such problems to some extent.

Decision crystallization. A second major activity for the new chair is *decision crystallization*. We discuss this challenging process in greater detail in Chapter 18. Basically, however, the process involves breaking big issues into smaller pieces, helping the group to discuss them piece by piece, "crystallizing" decisions by suggesting action, and working with the group to reach a decision. If the chair models this behavior, others will pick it up.

Preparation and timing are especially important for decision crystallization. If boards do not have adequate time to consider issues, then they will likely be forced into conservative, "Let's do it as we've done" procedures, practices, and decisions. Providing enough time to consider issues is an important first step toward changing and improving the board.

Interpersonal responsibilities

Although some of the responsibilities of the chair involve the development of ideas, others involve the development of people. There are several aspects to this role.

The first step is for the chair to understand that he or she has a development responsibility at all. *Development of people* means that the chair initiates programs and activities that, among other things, enable staff, the executive, and other directors to grow and improve, become more capable in their jobs, or take on more responsibilities. Being the chair is not just minding the store. It is improving the store.[1]

Chairpersons recognize this aspect of their leadership responsibilities differently. But without the growth and development of the agency's human capital, new programs will not have the talent and energy necessary for them to succeed. Energetic, developing people are prerequisites for energetic, developing programs. Each stimulates and is a requirement for the other.

The specifics of developing staff and directors are myriad. We discussed this role in Chapter 11. *Which* pro-

---

[1] People development is the responsibility of CEOs too, but many CEOs from both the nonprofit and corporate sectors do not see this aspect of their responsibilities either.

grams are in place is not as important as *whether* programs are in place. Whatever else the agency is, it should be a teaching institution, sharing vital new ideas and approaches and valid older ideas and approaches to all those who fall within its compass. Not only will the teaching role be helpful in and of itself, but the culture it creates will add quality to all agency programs.[2]

The responsibilities of the chair do not end with this kind of leadership. Other interpersonal tasks are involved as well. The chair should assist in developing a fun atmosphere within the agency. When the interpersonal climate is fun, people like to work with you, and you in turn gain a better staff and more from each staff member.

Additionally, the chair seeks to support specific directors in and out of board meetings. The chair protects those who are "underparticipating" and maintains some control over those who are "overparticipating." The chair sets the stage for evenhanded treatment of directors in and out of meetings. Overall, the chair tries to make the climate of the board meetings and the agency itself one of interpersonal value and strength. The goal is the development of the agency's human capital.

The Director

We have undertaken considerable discussion about the role of the chair because of the uncertainty and anxiety it generates. One cannot be a good chair, however, without having

---

[2] Teaching is important. We say this not because both of us have been teachers, but because the intellectual and organizational preparation for teaching focuses the mind and the organization. One person we interviewed said, "If your agency or organization does not do at least one thing so well [that] it can teach it to others, then it should go out of business!" That view may be a bit strong, but the point is well-taken.

good directors as members of the board. This seemingly innocuous role of director is the heart of the board. If the chair is the orchestra conductor, then the other board directors represent the orchestra itself. Thus, there are at least three tasks that the director should plan to perform well:

Review, review, review. Conduct a review of the agency, its mission, and purpose before accepting a nomination to the board. As is the case with the chair, people often accept invitations to serve as directors with little understanding of the nature of the enterprise in question, its stresses and strains, its history, or its potential conflicts. Indeed, to attract distinguished members, boards often minimize and occasionally even misrepresent such matters to potential directors. Only later, after the new director has actually joined the board, does he or she realize that the situation is not quite as originally presented. Thus, a certain amount of background—which includes a great deal of reading, as well as participating with the board in several joint projects—is absolutely essential. Consider the two-tier membership plan suggested in Chapter 3. Join a visiting committee, leadership circle, or advisory board for a year or so and see whether the nature of the organization; its mission and purpose; its operating style; and its policies, procedures, and practices suit your taste as a potential director.

Establish or update vision and mission. Look with some care at the existence or absence of a mission statement and strategic plan. Decision making—which is the essential job of boards—is difficult unless one has some overall sense of mission and purpose and the strategic direction in which the organization is moving. The new director, or any director, needn't agree with a particular strategic plan. Strategic plans can be changed, and frequently are. The absence of a plan, however, suggests a potential lack of thoughtfulness in an organization's decision making and a likelihood of ad hoc decisions based on constantly shifting forces. Potential directors should assure themselves that the organization has a decision-making framework in place.

Create good decision-making systems. Explore the reasonableness and thoroughness of decision-making procedures. Not only are mission statements and strategic plans necessary, but the appropriate mechanics for decision making must be in place or the organization will not be able to achieve its goals.

If the director-to-be has sufficient experience with the organization and is satisfied that the agency is on a desirable track, she or he can feel comfortable accepting the board position.

Once on the board, the director should observe at least five rules of thumb:

Do your homework. And do not lie about or misrepresent the extent to which you have actually done your homework. Quality decision making requires preparation. Without it, the discussion will not be of high quality, and the decision is not likely to be as good. If you are not prepared, keep a low profile at the meeting. Too frequently, directors who are unprepared to discuss particular issues will introduce extraneous matters into the board meeting, thus diverting the board's attention from a discussion for which everyone else has organized themselves.

Don't dump on the group. This occurs when the director raises a problem for which he or she does not offer a possible solution. Try, in all instances, to offer a solution to the problem you have raised. Even if you do not believe that yours should be the final solution, it can help get the discussion rolling. If you see a problem but cannot think of a particular solution, share that uncertainty with the group.

Aid the chair. Directors frequently blame the chair for rotten board meetings. Often, when the chair asks for input, directors avert their eyes or are hesitant to speak. Then, when the meeting breaks and everyone leaves for coffee, loud discussion occurs, almost as if by magic. Aiding the chair means chipping in occasionally when the chair asks; helping the chair control "overparticipators"; and, on occasion, inviting those who have not spoken to share their views. Too frequently after a board meeting, one director might say to a fellow director, "I know you have some great ideas on the topic. Why didn't you speak up?" Who knows? Perhaps the person was shy or needed to be encouraged. In any event, the time for that director to share his or her wisdom has passed. Aiding the chair means helping the chairperson make the meeting go well while the meeting is in progress.

Use supportive communication. Being a director involves open and supportive communication within the board context. At one level, this means controlling one's body language, especially indications of disfavor. Observers at board meetings frequently report looks of disgust, head shaking, and whispering to others as proposals are discussed. This indirect communication often fails, because no one is quite sure how to read it. Nonetheless, it creates a negative atmosphere and discourages other directors from making suggestions and proposals for fear of the scorn that may be indirectly heaped upon them. More direct, straightforward statements of agreement or disagreement are more effective and can clear the air.

Be loyal to the board. Directors frequently differ on policy matters. Individuals win and lose on policies that are important to them. Sometimes, one loses on a policy proposal that later turns out to have been the correct road the board should have taken. Keep discussions and criticisms of the group within the group's boundaries, particularly within the boundaries of the board meetings. No one likes people who seek to establish their own presence by criticizing board decisions to others. Although critics may believe they are enhancing their own status, they're really only diminishing their status in the eyes of their fellow directors.

With these behaviors in mind, the director's role should be a productive one. While these are difficult tasks, understanding them is a good first step.

The Executive Director

The executive director or president of the organization is often an ex officio member of the board. This ex officio status was clearer when agencies used the title *executive director* almost exclusively. In that case, a lay board of citizen volunteers founded or supervised some kind of helpful enterprise called a social agency. They hired an administrator—the executive director—to do the administrative work and to participate, by ex officio status, in forming the agency's policy. The executive director was—and, for the most part, remains—a nonvoting member of the board, although he or she may have had substantial informal influence through personal contacts and participation at meetings. In corporate parlance, executive directors of human service organizations were "outside directors."

As we said in Chapter 1, however, this practice is changing, so we are now in a state of flux. The titles *president* and *chief executive officer*, or *CEO*, are increasingly the norm. We have to be sure, therefore, that we're all talking about the same person. In this book, we use *executive director* or simply *executive*. Whatever the term, we are referring to the senior paid official—not a volunteer—employed by the

zation to carry out its policies. What is most impor-
_ ₁₃ that the board establishes a clear definition of that
person's role.

In addition to being, as we have said, a nonvoting member of the board (although this practice may vary in some specific context), the executive director today provides a number of important services for the board of directors. First, she or he acts in an administrative function by staffing the board, orchestrating the preparation of agenda materials for meetings; assisting the board, its executive committee, and the other committees in carrying out their functions; synthesizing and organizing materials; and, on occasion, assisting committees in actually writing documents. The board should establish guidelines to avoid using the executive's time capriciously.

The executive director performs a substantive function for the board as well. Typically, an executive director is hired because of his or her substantive expertise in the areas of the agency's mission. The executive can apprise the board regularly about developments in the field. In a sense, the executive director serves an educational function for the board, both collectively and individually. Again, the board may choose to delegate some aspects of these tasks, lest they become too time consuming, considering there is only one executive but frequently many directors.

As we said in Chapter 10, a delicate balance must be maintained between the board and the executive director. Typically, one thinks of the board as responsible for policy and the executive director for administration, but obviously there is an important gray area where these two realms intersect. Most central is the relationship between the executive director and the board chair. They are, respectively, the organization's chief paid administrative and volunteer lay officials. Their relationship is critical, and they should meet with each other regularly, sharing perspectives and views,

not only about specific proposals un
but also about the organization's genera.
orientation.

Evaluation of the executive director occ
guidance of the chair. Executive directors frequ
that they just get a new chair "broken in" when
leaves and a new one takes over. Although it i
overly formal, an early meeting between the execu
the chair, even going so far as establishing a written i..
of agreement about areas of interest and activity, can go
far toward preventing conflicts that can threaten the
organization's productivity and morale.

Ultimate Responsibility

When all is said and done, the final responsibility for the
organization ultimately rests with the board of directors.
This is an important truth, even though the executive director surely devotes much time and energy toward developing particular services and orientations and may hold
strong opinions about specific matters before the board.
Indeed, the board may not always accept the executive's
recommendations, and that may sometimes mean that the
board makes incorrect decisions. Nonetheless, the overall
wisdom in the field is that, in the long run, an independent,
volunteer board of directors produces the best decisions.

This view has been supported in recent years. Consider
the many examples of the relatively self-serving conduct by
corporate boards. The organizational interests of inside
members did not give them sufficient breadth of view and
independence of perspective to take the necessary actions
that could have prevented many sectors of American
industry from becoming deeply troubled.

ercise 11
Assessment of Board Roles

Area of Responsibility	Assessment			
Chair	Yes	Somewhat	Not a Great Deal	Don't Know
Is prepared for chair role	❏	❏	❏	❏
Preacceptance				
Has statesperson perspective	❏	❏	❏	❏
Has assessed other directors	❏	❏	❏	❏
Has negotiated conditions for appointment	❏	❏	❏	❏
Has performed self-assessment	❏	❏	❏	❏
Operational responsibilities	Often	Sometimes	Hardly Ever	Don't Know
Clarifies expectations with executive	❏	❏	❏	❏
Agrees with executive on overall strategy and goals	❏	❏	❏	❏
Establishes working relationship with executive	❏	❏	❏	❏
Meets regularly with executive	❏	❏	❏	❏

Area of Responsibility		*Assessment*		
Intellectual responsibilities	Often	Sometimes	Hardly Ever	Don't Know
Establishes policy agenda	❏	❏	❏	❏
Helps to crystallize decisions	❏	❏	❏	❏
Uses discussion	❏	❏	❏	❏
Uses decrystallization to prevent premature closure	❏	❏	❏	❏
Interpersonal responsibilities				
Recognizes role of developing people	❏	❏	❏	❏
Helps others to grow	❏	❏	❏	❏
Develops fun atmosphere	❏	❏	❏	❏
Provides support for directors	❏	❏	❏	❏

Director	Yes/ Often	Somewhat/ Sometimes	Not a Great Deal/ Hardly Ever	Don't Know
Assessed agency background before acceptance	❏	❏	❏	❏
Checks strategic planning	❏	❏	❏	❏
Reviews decision-making procedures	❏	❏	❏	❏

Area of Responsibility		*Assessment*		
Director (cont.)	Yes/ Often	Somewhat/ Sometimes	Not a Great Deal/ Hardly Ever	Don't Know
Does homework	❏	❏	❏	❏
Doesn't dump on group	❏	❏	❏	❏
Aids the chair	❏	❏	❏	❏
Participates openly	❏	❏	❏	❏
Is loyal to the board	❏	❏	❏	❏

Executive Director

Clear definition of role established	❏	❏	❏	❏
Staffs the board	❏	❏	❏	❏
Provides the board with substantive knowledge	❏	❏	❏	❏
Has good working relationship with chair	❏	❏	❏	❏
Recognizes board has final responsibility for the organization	❏	❏	❏	❏

Chapter 13

Assessment and Evaluation

Assessment helps the board work well. Before one can improve something, one must first assess its current condition. Individual directors, board decisions, and indeed the direction of the entire organization should be assessed. But evaluation is always uncomfortable, and for that reason people resist it.

When considering evaluation, bear in mind that

- Assessment and evaluation do not seek to assign blame. Evaluation is like watching game films. The team must continually assess its progress.

- Improvement is a process—a journey—and assessment is where that journey begins. Individuals and groups alike are nearly always interested in improving themselves, and evaluation should become a part of the organization's culture as improvement itself.

- Organizations should try different approaches to evaluation—individual, group, organizational, programmatic, and others. Many measures are better than one.

- All evaluations and assessments begin with goals. Without expectations to serve as benchmarks, no assessment is possible. This means the organization must have such items as a strategic plan, job descriptions for its directors, and explicit annual plans for the executive, among others.

- Evaluation is the first step toward development. If the organization does not know where it is, it cannot plan how to get where it wants to go.

Assessing Directors

Each individual director serving on the board should receive an annual evaluation. This idea runs counter to some thinking; after all, volunteers are not paid, and, besides, the prospect of an evaluation might discourage one from volunteering in the first place. But, a director, like any volunteer, commits to the role. A volunteer's commitment is no less important than any other. Hence, evaluation of how the director performs in that role is necessary.

Why is evaluation of directors important?

- It emphasizes the seriousness of the director's role. The roles that no one looks at are the ones that no one cares about, paid or unpaid. Far from making the director's role less attractive, the very fact of evaluation emphasizes its importance.
- Evaluation helps get the job done. When we know we will be evaluated, we are more likely to do the job than if no one ever looks or asks. Hence, the very presence of evaluation, regardless of the method, is an incentive to complete assigned tasks.
- Evaluation of individual directors becomes a vehicle for overall organizational assessment. The information, when compiled, provides the organization as a whole a sense of its decision-making performance.
- Evaluating directors sends a message to staff—who often believe that directors do whatever directors want and that no one holds directors accountable,

Am I a Good Director?

Reflect on how you have contributed to the board.
Consider such things as

- ☐ regularity of attendance
- ☐ preparation for meetings
- ☐ willingness to play "task" roles (pushing for goal achievement)
- ☐ willingness to play "process" roles (encouraging and soothing others)
- ☐ ability and willingness to support change
- ☐ ability and willingness to support innovation

If the board desires, it can assign a numeric scale to these items so they can be scored.

Write a paragraph critiquing your own board performance, and propose specific ways in which you plan to improve. Share this with other directors.

while the staff does the real work of the agency and is always under scrutiny—that all members of the team are, in fact, accountable.

Directors' performance, then, along with overall board performance and the performance of other personnel, should be evaluated regularly as part of an organizational assessment system. We have already introduced some ideas about evaluation and assessment in Chapter 12. As we have said repeatedly throughout this book, an assessment system must begin with developing job descriptions and descriptions of goals and missions. Without that initial step, at the individual or organizational level, examining performance is meaningless.

Who should perform the evaluation? Organizations could follow a couple of different approaches. One, of course, is self-evaluation; the example on page 137 can be used in this way. Self-serving self-reports are a possibility, however. The very best method is a three-way approach: Each individual director completes the "Am I a Good Director?" worksheet, but the executive director and the other board members also use this form to evaluate each other. The board can assign numeric scales to the evaluation so that each area can be scored. These scores are averaged and presented to all directors at a board meeting. A consultant could do the averaging to ensure anonymity when directors are evaluating each other. This three-way approach gives directors a feel for the views of their board colleagues, as well as their own.

Evaluating Decisions

Boards of directors have products—their decisions. Boards must ask themselves, "Are our products—the decisions we make—any good?" Without evaluation, the board is not likely to have the feedback necessary to sustain quality decisions. Evaluating the board's decision making requires two tools: decision audits and decision autopsies.

The Decision Audit

The board appoints a committee of three directors to review and grade its decisions. The auditing committee extracts a year's worth of decisions from the board's minutes. This information will be easily available if the board follows the Rule of Minutes detailed in Chapter 16. The most recent decision should have occurred about six months prior to the decision audit to allow the auditing committee to make fair observations as to how the decision has worked. Each auditor grades the decisions according to a scale:

A The A decision is one in which, in the judgment of the auditors, all parties to the decision were winners. This is an "all-win" or a "win-win" decision: Everyone affected by the decision must have come out ahead—although everyone does not have to come out equally ahead.

B The B decision is one in which there were some winners and some losers. It is a "some-win" decision; but, on balance, the outcome is positive.

C The C decision results in some winners and losers but the win-lose balance is about equal. The C decision is a "win-lose" decision—there are both losses and gains, but they tend to cancel each other out.

D The D decision is the opposite of a B—some wins, some losses; but, on balance, more losses than gains.

F The F decision might also be called the "no-win" or "nuclear war" decision. No one wins, and all are further behind after the decision than they were before.

When grading decisions based on their outcomes, auditors should give special attention to and differentiate between the decision process and the implementation process. Poor outcomes could result from either, but the changes necessary would be different.

The auditors compare their individual ratings for patterns and areas of agreement or disagreement among themselves. Decisions that all three grade as As or as Ds or Fs should be set aside for decision autopsies. Patterns of divergent grading for the same decision—for example, if one auditor gives a decision an A and another gives the same decision a C—most likely reveal that the auditors are using different bases to assess the decisions. The discrepancy itself should become a subject for the board to consider.

The Decision Autopsy

Before reporting their findings to the board, the auditors should conduct a decision autopsy. This is simply an intensive examination of one pair of decisions, one graded as an A and the other as a D or F. Naturally, when one does something right, as in an A decision, one should analyze the decision and how it can be repeated. Similarly, but more painfully, in the case of a bad decision, one should find out what went wrong and how it can be prevented.

Reporting to the board on the good work behind an A decision has the added benefit of praising directors for their efforts. Auditors should bear in mind, however, that, on the downside, the board is likely to be defensive toward a review of poor or failed decisions. This defensiveness is blunted in part—but only in part—by praise for the A decision.

Decision autopsies in which we have been involved have revealed common patterns of difficulty among D and F decisions. Some of the most frequent causes of bad board decisions include:

- The board was under pressure to make a decision quickly, as in a crisis.
- The board had inadequate information to make its decision.
- The board was intolerant of independent or different views when making its decision.

- The decision was the result of coercion or group-think (see Chapter 14) or premature or improper agreement on a restricted set of alternative decisions.

These are among the most common reasons why bad decisions happen; we offer more reasons and examples in the next chapter.

Once the decision-auditing committee completes both its audit and the decision autopsy, it is ready to report to the board on the grading of the board's decisions in the last year; divergent areas in the auditors' gradings, which the board should discuss; and the results of the decision autopsy.

Operations Assessment

Boards must also evaluate the economy and appropriateness of their agencies' operations. This first requires that the board establish the total resources, in terms of personnel and money, available to carry out the organization's tasks. With this as a base, the board can look at how the agency's resources are allocated. One way to approach this task is through the *professional unit method of analysis*. This method works well for agencies and their boards in strategic planning efforts, as well as for executives in terms of developing materials and staff assignments [see Tropman & Tropman 1995].

To conduct a professional unit analysis, the board must first develop a professional unit of service that is simple enough to allow all directors to understand the process, yet complete enough to be useful. This unit is the *worker week*. The analysis then proceeds as follows:

- The executive director, and perhaps a small committee of directors, calculates the number of direct
service workers available to the agency. Consider
only those who perform the actual work of the
agency; do not include those who do administration, supervision, janitorial work, clerical tasks, or
similar duties. In a clinical service agency, this
would be the number of clinicians, up to and
including fractional amounts (for example, one-
third of so-and-so's job relates to clinical work).
In a planning agency, it would be the number of
junior and senior planners. These are *direct service
workers;* other workers are support staff. Even the
executive, unless she or he sees clients or spends
some time reviewing planning reports or policy
documents, is considered support staff. For the
purposes of our example, we will assume the
agency has 10 direct service staff.

- Calculate the number of weeks of work available
to the direct service staff to perform the agency's
work. In calculations we have done in trials, the
approximate number turns out to be around 45 or
46 weeks out of the total 52 in a year. This ac-
counts for such things as holidays, vacation, and
sick leave. To simplify the multiplication in our
example, let's assume the agency executive and
board has 50 weeks of staff time per worker for
whatever tasks the agency undertakes.

- Multiply the number of workers by the total number of weeks. In our example, the agency ends up
with 500 worker weeks for all agency programs
and activities.

- Divide the number of worker weeks into the total agency budget. This gives the total dollar amount per worker week. If we assume our agency budget is $500,000, then the total amount of money per worker week is $1,000.

The board and the executive can now use this material in any number of analyses. For example, dividing the total dollar amount per worker week by the number of the agency's programs, the executive can review with directors agency's priorities. Human service agencies, as well as other organizations, commonly experience organizational "drift," wherein agency allocations, personnel, and resources move slowly from desired goals to other objectives. One can measure this drift using staff time records. If kept accurately, these records can reveal much about time allocation.

Organizational drift is the rule rather than the exception. A variety of informal and historical factors can cause organizational drift, and it frequently goes unnoticed. A strategic assessment would note such a reallocation and allow the agency to correct or redirect its course. Too, the agency may be doing exactly what it is supposed to be doing according to its goals and objectives, but, upon review, the agency determines that its goals and objectives are inappropriate to the needs of the community. Here again, the professional unit method of analysis allows the board to see the overall allocation of effort more clearly, in terms of both personnel and dollars.

The professional unit method of analysis fuses dollars and people into a single, easily comprehensible unit. Boards think more in terms of people than money, but much of their planning and decision making is often done in terms of disembodied monetary units, removing it from the reality of human services. The professional unit method of analysis allows a crisper, cleaner approach to strategic thinking. After all, once an organization determines its objectives, it has to begin allocating staff and budgetary resources. The professional unit method of analysis offers a clear view of what the organization is doing and what it might be doing, and a factual basis for determining whether its activities correspond with its objectives.

Strategic Drift and Strategic Centering

Lastly, the agency needs to look at strategic drift and strategic centering. Is it placing its resources where its goals are? To answer this question, the agency must compare what it is really doing with what it would like to be doing or what it is supposed to be doing.

Here, the *drift index,* or *index of dissimilarity,* is useful. It provides a numerical value measuring the difference between the organization's actual activities and assignment of staff on one hand and its desired activities and assignments on the other. The agency can conduct this assessment in a variety of ways, but the index is a relatively quick yet sophisticated measure that provides lots of information for minimum effort. It builds on the professional unit method of analysis.

Once the executive or a planning committee has developed a professional unit analysis, the directors fill out a small questionnaire, as suggested in the sample at right. The questionnaire is simply a list of the major organizational activities or programs. Directors are asked to allocate the percentage of organizational time they feel should go to

Index of Dissimilarity, or Drift Index

Questionnaire for Directors

Please indicate the percentage of time you believe the agency should be spending on each goal or activity.

Specific Goal or Activity #1   _____

Specific Goal or Activity #2   _____

Specific Goal or Activity #3   _____

Specific Goal or Activity #4   _____

Innovation (fixed item @ 15%)   15%

Individual Item   _____   _____

Individual Item   _____   _____

TOTAL   100%

Note: Give this questionnaire to each director, and, if you wish, to all staff as well. Average the responses and list on a feedback sheet for the board. Board and staff responses can be combined or, better yet, create two feedback sheets—one with board values and one with staff averages.

each activity. The questionnaire also includes several blank lines that allow them to propose activities that the organization does not currently undertake.

The planning committee or executive averages the directors' allocations for these activities and inserts the averages in Column A, on the Drift Index Worksheet (shown on page 147). The percentages of time for what the agency is actually doing, derived from professional unit analysis, go in Column B. Thus, Column A represents the ideal, Column B the reality. Column C represents the difference, subtracting B from A (disregarding the sign, or converting negative amounts to positives). The percentage differences in Column C are then added and divided by two. The resulting number is the *drift index,* or *index of dissimilarity,* and quantifies the difference between what the organization is actually doing and what it wants to do.

The index provides terrific factual information that the board can use to refocus, redirect, and reinspire the organization. The percentages are easily converted back into professional units, so directors can quickly see what their percent of effort means in terms of percent of budget allocation. Indeed, instead of professional units, the drift index worksheet can also use actual budget fractions in Columns A and B.

Percentage allocations clarify the choice process. Directors don't always have a broad sense of organizational allocations. They often talk in terms of placing more emphasis on one area and less on another. Forcing the choice by use of a percentage mechanism pinpoints differences in approach and emphasis.

The drift index quickly reveals one deficiency of most organizations. Many allocate nothing for innovation, new programs, or experimental work. Absolutely everything is consumed by operating programs. It is tough to become an entrepreneurial board if there are no resources at all for new and innovative programs. We suggested a guideline in Chapter 7 that 15% of the organization's resources be targeted toward innovation. This item and percent are fixed in the examples in this chapter. This goal may take three

Drift Index Worksheet

Percentage Use of Time, Budget, or Professional Units

Operational Goals or Activities	*Column A* Average Ideal %	*Column B* Actual %	*Column C* Difference A - B*
1. Residential Treatment	50	40	10
2. Counseling	15	30	15
3. Home Care	10	10	0
4. Individual Item			
Innovation	15	0	15
Miscellaneous	10	20	10
TOTALS	100	100	50
Sum of Column C ÷ 2			50/2
Drift Index			25%

* Disregard signs (i.e., convert negative sums to positive amounts)

years to reach if the board is not presently targeting any resources toward innovation.

The drift index is extremely flexible. The executive can use it with staff to compare the executive's assignment of work load with the staff's actual percentage allocations. As the beginning of a strategic process, either at the board level or within the organization, the technique is a good start.

The Key to Success

Assessment and evaluation are crucial to the successful board. For the excellent board, evaluation becomes second nature to its operation. Assessment and evaluation must take place in four areas: the performance of individual directors, the board's policy decisions, the organization's operations, and the possibility of mission drift. Of these, evaluating the board's decision making may be the most critical. Because policy decisions are the central product of the board, improving them is a central feature of the directors' responsibilities.

Exercise 12

Does your board have an evaluation policy?

If so, can it be improved?

If not, can one be developed?

Complete the Drift Index Exercise at right.

Drift Index Exercise

Write down your organization's mission statement.

Now list, in priority order, a set of operational goals derived from the strategic plan. Insert these on Lines 1–6 of the worksheet. If you have more, adapt this worksheet as necessary. Using the sample Drift Index Worksheet on page 147 as an example, complete this worksheet for your organization.

Operational Goals or Activities	*Column A* Average Ideal %	*Column B* Actual %	*Column C* Difference A - B*
1. _____	_____	_____	_____
2. _____	_____	_____	_____
3. _____	_____	_____	_____
4. _____	_____	_____	_____
5. _____	_____	_____	_____
6. _____	_____	_____	_____
Innovation	15	_____	_____
TOTALS	100	100	_____
Sum of Column C ÷ 2			x/2
Drift Index			%

* Disregard signs (i.e., convert negative sums to positive amounts)

Part IV

How to Do It: The Board Meeting

"The board is in agreement, then—rock and roll will never die."

Part IV

How to Do It:
The Board Meeting

Overview

Nearly everything we have talked about thus far needs to happen—at least in part—within the context of the board meeting. Great meetings are conditions of great boards. Without running an effective meeting, the board cannot carry out its responsibilities, and it cannot use the tools we have discussed.

Let's look at what can go wrong in board meetings and consider how to set these problems right.

Chapter 14

Making High-Quality Decisions

The board of directors as a group, and directors as individuals, cannot accomplish the tasks we have discussed in this manual unless the board meetings, and the processes surrounding the development of board meetings, are effective and efficient. A casual meeting that approximates a social gathering and does not attend to the items at hand in a serious way will not only produce decisions of inferior quality but may also leave the board's decisions open for judicial review. This applies to committee meetings as well, as they, too, are part of the overall process. What are some common problems of board meetings?

What Goes Wrong

Board meetings have many potential pitfalls. They often start late, can go on too long, and frequently accomplish little or nothing. You may have your own list of problems. Much has been written about group decision making, and experts have identified some common decision problems and pitfalls.

Decision avoidance occurs when agencies put off necessary decisions until the very last minute, or even after the last minute. One form of this malady is the "nondecision." A decision may appear to have been made, but it really has not been. Things go along very much as they have. Over

155

time, this pattern of nondecision can lead to the "boiled frog phenomenon" [Tichy & Devanna 1990]. As we explained in Chapter 7, if one puts a frog in a petri dish filled with water and slowly heats the water over a Bunsen burner, the frog will not jump out, and it eventually boils to death. Why does it not leave? Apparently, the just-noticeable differ-ence in the temperature is never enough to cause action. This just-noticeable difference phenomenon is an impor-tant source of nondecision in organizations. Directors see things pretty much as they were, so they never see a need to act.

Decision randomness, or the "garbage can model," is a second problem. Cohen, March, and Olsen [1972] argue that organizations and their boards usually include four types of personalities: *problem knowers* (people who know the difficulties the organization faces); *solution providers* (people who can provide solutions but do not know the problems); *resource controllers* (people who do not know the problems and do not have solutions but control the allocation of people and money in the organization); and *decision makers looking for work* (those who are ready for decision opportunities). For effective decision making, all four elements must be in the same room at the same time. In reality, most organizations combine them at random, as if tossing them into a garbage can. No wonder bad decisions result.

Decision deflection, or the "Abilene Paradox," [Harvey 1974] is another scenario of bad decision making. A group of people are outside the town of Abilene, Texas, with nothing to do. Somehow, they wind up going into town— a hot, dusty drive of many miles with no air conditioning— to have a very bad meal. On the way back, the "search for guilty parties" begins as the group tries to figure out whose idea it was to undertake this wholly unstatisfying road trip. The Abilene Paradox has come to refer to group actions undertaken with no real decision to do so.

Decision coercion, also known as groupthink, is yet another well-known decision problem [Janis 1972, 1983]. In groupthink, board decisions capitulate to power. One kind of power is group cohesion. In very cohesive groups, there is a coming together—not an agreement on the issues, but rather a strong wish to maintain the cohesion of the group. This commitment to the group sometimes means that no one really explores alternatives or considers options, because that might cause differences within the group, potentially harming cohesion. Decisions, therefore, are made too quickly. A second kind of decision coercion involves a powerful director, chair, or CEO. When such a leader says, "We're all agreed then," most at the table say, "Aye." Only later, in the hallway, when the real discussions occur, do problems surface.

Meetings—all kinds of meetings—are an unpleasant topic in American society. Generally, the jokes that people tell about boards and committees refer to their ineptitude and inability to accomplish social purposes. "Boards," so the joke goes, "are forests of dead wood." "Committees (or boards) take minutes and waste hours." The humor goes on. To achieve more effective meetings, we first must understand why things go wrong.

Why Things Go Wrong

Meetings go wrong for lots of reasons. We stress here some key ones, as they may not leap immediately to mind. Since many individual directors have lots of meetings in other aspects of their lives, they think they "know" about meetings. In all likelihood, they are really not aware of some key problems.

Contrary values. Boards and committees, as examples of group life, tend to be contrary to American values. Zander [1982] says it best:

> Readers face a dilemma...[we] are not all that interested in explaining or improving group life.... Individuals feel that the organization should help them; it is not the individual's prime job to help the organization.... Basic values...foster the formation of groups that put the good of the individual before the good of the group. In Japan, in contrast, important values foster interdependence among persons, courtesy, obligation to others, listening, empathy, self-denial, and support of one's group. [p. xi]

We like to do things individually; improving group decision making requires extra effort.

Hidden functions. Another reason for why things go wrong relates to a number of hidden functions that boards and committees perform—such as representing the community or providing a voice for those whose voices cannot be heard otherwise. Hidden functions flow from expectations that people have about boards. Some believe boards should "represent" all of the positions and groups in the community. Some see boards as vehicles for social justice and social action, while others see them in more narrow, organizational terms. These expectations often surface around decisions, processes, procedures, and outcomes, causing conflict and decision delay.

Lack of training. Because of the problems of group life in general and in board and committee life in particular, group members tend not to be prepared for group roles. Group members often suffer from a simple lack of knowing what to do. Remedies, such as this manual, are all too rare.

Lack of preparation. Finally, for all of the above reasons, directors tend not to prepare themselves well for meetings, taking instead a casual, "let the chips fall where they may" approach. Material is often late and either inadequate or overadequate. Directors tend to not attend meetings regularly, and they do not always read the material when they do attend. To counter this trend, the board often reviews material at the meeting, which offends those who have prepared, and so it goes. Meetings become one disappointment after another; for this reason, many directors consider any investment in preparation to be a waste of time.

Self-fulfilling prophecy. These four reasons combine to create self-fulfilling prophecy that almost ensures board meetings of poor quality. Since group members don't believe in meetings; since groups often perform a range of obscure and hidden functions; and since members have neither the training nor take the time to prepare for meetings, group meetings are likely to go badly. This experience results in an inappropriate generalization about meetings. We come to believe that something inherent about meetings makes them go badly. The evidence of rotten meetings only reinforces the original presupposition. This reinforcement, in turn, convinces directors that efforts to improve meetings are a waste of time. And this conclusion virtually ensures increased difficulty in the meeting itself. Once this cycle starts, meeting quality spirals downward.

A Recipe for Improvement

The problems with meetings are more than mere annoyances. They lead to bad decisions that can result in poor service to those in need, make the agency an awful place to work, and ultimately cause the agency's demise.

Discussing why things go wrong sets the stage for a recipe that can help make things go right. As with all recipes, the ingredients must be applied promptly and together. One can't sprinkle a little bit here and there and expect things to come out in a good fashion. What this means for the board of directors is a systematic and planned approach to improving meeting quality. The next chapter shows you how.

Exercise 13

Grade your board meetings (A = Excellent, B = Good, C = Average, D = Poor, F = Failure). To get an A, your meetings have to have three features: Decisions are made in a timely fashion, decisions are of high quality, and people have fun and enjoy themselves.

Consider some problems with your board meetings. List them here.

Chapter 15

Seven Key Principles for Effective Board Meetings

How can we make things go better in meetings? Many of the people we interviewed about governance shared some of the approaches they use. We called these people "meeting masters," and their board meetings share three characteristics:

- decisions get made;
- decisions are of high quality; and
- members have fun.

How they managed to accomplish this, we detail here. Their techniques can be applied to any meeting, not just board meetings.[1]

If board meetings are to be improved—and they can and should be—then we need principles for a new kind of meeting structure. These principles form an important base for thinking about how meetings can be improved.

The Orchestra Principle

Board meetings should be like an orchestra performance: They should be at the end of a process of development and preparation rather than at its beginning. No decent orchestra would simply stroll onstage and begin playing. Rather,

---

[1] For a general discussion of meetings, see Tropman 1996a.

the orchestra chooses its musical selections, holds rehearsals, and procures the proper soloists and accompanists. An orchestra would look very funny performing a piano concerto with no pianist. It would be even funnier if the conductor said, "Ladies and gentlemen, please excuse me, but the oboist has to leave early tonight. We know you'll understand. Unfortunately, the last piece on our program has an oboe solo in it. Therefore, we're going to ask the oboist to play those notes right now. Then, if you could kindly remember them when we get to the oboe section of the last piece, it would be a favor to us all. Thank you."

How often is this scene repeated in board meetings? The chair gets up and says, "Excuse me, but Sheila has to leave early. Therefore, we'd like to go directly to her business," regardless of the nature or complexity of that business or its position in the structure of the meeting itself. If directors can think of the meeting like an orchestra performance and apply the rules of quality and structure that one would apply to such a performance, we are already moving toward improved board meetings.

The "No More Reports" Principle

Reports have become the enemy of many board meetings. Frequently, boards have numerous standing committees, each of which is invited to report at every board meeting, regardless of whether the committee has any actual pending business. Board meetings have become oral newsletters—and thus the minutes have turned into actual newsletters. Under the Three Characters Principle, below, all reports are culled in advance as information, action, or discussion items. These items are then scheduled at appropriate places on the meeting agenda.

The "No More Reports" Principle thus contains two interrelated but crucial elements. First, unless the committee has specific business, no report is scheduled. Rather, an announcement of committee activity is attached to the meeting announcement. Second, and perhaps more importantly, reports are disaggregated into their parts. Rather than having a treasurer's report, for example, which may contain items for decision, some for discussion, and still others for information, those items are distributed in appropriate places on the agenda. The treasurer, therefore, may appear three times on the agenda, once during the announcement stage, second during the decision stage, and finally during the discussion stage.

Does this kind of structure seem odd? Applying the orchestra principle, it's certainly no odder than having the oboist appear at several points where the oboe is called for. No one would seriously recommend that a particular instrument get up and play all the notes for that instrument at one particular point during the performance simply for the convenience of the performer. Yet we routinely schedule for the treasurer or some other committee chair a large batch of unrelated items merely for his or her convenience.

Of course, the items are not totally unrelated; in the case of the treasurer, for example, they all apply to money. What is important here is not only their substantive link, but also their action imperatives—announcement, discussion, or decision.

The "No New Business" Principle

New business is another enemy of board meetings. This may come as a shock and surprise. Board chairs frequently tell us, "We don't know what the directors want to talk about until they get to the meeting, do we?" Well, not unless we ask them. And indeed, that is one of the most important rules for running effective meetings. Finding out in advance what items are coming up for discussion is imperative, because only in that way can one be sure that the information and people germane to that discussion are present. Without adequate information, people tend to substitute stereotypic information: "What we all know is true." Discussions around new business are typically the most unprofitable in any board meeting. We are usually ignorant of new business items, but our ignorance does not keep us from participating in the discussion. Rather, it seems to increase our desire to say something—anything—regardless of how ridiculous it may appear in retrospect.

The Principle of Proactivity

New business is often introduced under a cloud of pressure. An executive or board chair will come into a meeting and indicate that an item is up for discussion and decision but that action must be taken immediately because of one pressure or another. Without question, pressure is the enemy of high-quality decisions. Under pressure, clarity and quality of thought seem to decrease, evidence becomes sparse, emotion and table pounding replace the absent evidence, and the board takes a series of problematic decision-making steps.

Retrospective analysis of decisions that have gone terribly sour almost always indicate that an early step was made under conditions of great pressure. This kind of decision is reactive in nature. Major outlines of what must be done are already in place—put there by the environment, or outside funders, or similar forces. Directors have very limited options, and these limitations are usually the source of the pressure.

We need to move toward proactive decisions and a decision-making style that anticipates environmental developments and tries to deal with them at an appropriate distance—not too far away, because then the issue seems unreal, nor too close, because then pressure makes solutions too difficult. A midpoint of distance works best for proactivity.

The Three Characters Principle

Only three kinds of business occur in board meetings— announcements, decisions, and discussion. Nothing else goes on. But we often schedule these items in disregard of their character, thus whipping the directors from an announcement to a decision then to another announcement, then to a discussion, and so on. The board becomes hopelessly lost. And, frequently, the exact character of the item is not identified, so some directors think they are hearing about it, others want to decide it, and still others want to discuss but not decide. Of course, this confusion among the directors means there is confusion in the meeting, if not chaos.

Under the Three Characters Principle, the agenda items are identified in advance as

- announcements,
- decision items, or
- matters requiring discussion or brainstorming.

All items of a similar character should be handled at the same time in the meeting, and in this order:

announcements, decisions, and discussion-brainstorming items. This facilitates group interaction and allows for orderly progression from one type of item to another.

The Rule of Two-Thirds and the Rule of the Agenda Bell, in Chapter 16, build on the Three Characters Principle.

The Role Principle

We often hear that a board's problems are the result of the personality or personalities of one or more directors. People have spoken to us about "getting rid" of certain "troublesome" directors. Directors have told us that the reason their board meetings are bad is because of the "mental illness" of individual directors and offer as evidence ample illustrations of "crazy behavior" by the directors in question. Individual directors are often typed or characterized by aspects of their personalities: Arthur Angry, Tillie Talk-a-Lot, and Sam Stall all make frequent appearances on boards of directors.

Such diagnoses are a result of our individualistic presuppositions. As a society, we tend to view deficits in procedures and functions in terms of the characteristics and personalities of the individuals performing those procedures and functions. This book, however, has stressed the importance of examining the roles themselves, rather than the people filling the roles, in strengthening and improving functions, procedures, and rules. These repairs alone will make a substantial difference in the quality of meetings and will enable us to rethink our diagnoses of insanity on the part of individual directors.

More often than not, the person is playing a role scripted by the norms of the group. Consider "Jim," for example.

As a new director, Jim applied his habit of arriving on time for meetings. But he soon noticed that this board started meetings very late; before long, he was coming late as well. Older directors started to comment, "It's too bad about Jim. We hoped he would come on time, but he's just like the rest of us!" Talk about blaming the victim! These seven new principles, the 10 new rules we propose in Chapter 16, and the three new roles outlined in Chapter 17 will help rescript board meetings.

The Principle of Quality Decisions

In the final analysis, boards of directors are after decisions of high quality. Quality decisions do not just happen, any more than excellence in any kind of performance—sports, acting, music—simply occurs. When we observe such outstanding or excellent performances, they often appear to be flawless, easy, even simplistic. Yet anyone who has ever tried to saw his or her way through a violin concerto, or sink a 20-foot putt, or cast a fishing fly in exactly the right place understands the months and years of practice that go into such flawless performances. Board decisions must be approached with care, not casualness. When approached with care, the decision, as a "performance," is not only likely to be of high quality in and of itself, but is also likely to be part of a pattern of high-quality decisions, which in turn result from a decision-making system of high quality.

Seven Principles Applied

Board meetings are the central engine through which boards conduct business. Preparation is necessary, of course; materials have to be developed for the meeting. But if the meeting is not well-run, then all the preparation and commitments of the volunteers—the directors—are wasted. The first step is a paradigm shift, to start thinking differently about the basic structure of board meetings. That is what these new principles do. Chapter 16 offers a recipe for planning board meetings, and Chapter 17 discusses the positions and roles in board meetings.

Chapter 16

Ten Key Rules for Effective Board Meetings

Boards of directors must think long and hard about how to improve their meeting process—a prescription that applies, as well, to meetings within the organization itself and meetings in which the organization joins with others in community efforts. The rules here are driven by information. Without that information, it's hard to make good decisions. The cumulative focus of these 10 rules, therefore, is to follow up on items that need information, focus the information required for any decision items on the meeting agenda, and transmit that information to the board in an understandable, timely fashion so the board can act on it.

The Rule of Halves

The first rule is a simple agenda matter. It asserts that all items for an upcoming meeting must be in the hands of the agenda scheduler one-half of the time between meetings. Thus, for a monthly board meeting, the agenda scheduler should receive all agenda items two weeks before the next meeting. All directors should have an opportunity to contribute to the agenda to ensure that the agenda is built from the concerns of the directors, not issued as some standard template.

The agenda scheduler is usually the executive or the chair; sometimes, the two work together. A frequent pattern is for the executive to put together a draft agenda, then check it with the chair. This arrangement is fine, as long as the executive examines all of the items closely, screens out those that could be handled outside of the board meeting, sifts through them for items that are too big and should be broken down or too small and should be packaged with other items, and assesses the items with respect to the availability of information. There's very little point in scheduling an item if the information required for a decision is not available. Sometimes the executive needs to check with directors and staff members who are working on or otherwise involved with issues that show up as potential agenda items. Checking with them in advance is a courtesy as well as a help.

The Rule of Sixths

Once the agenda scheduler—let's assume that it is the executive—has assembled a list of potential agenda items, they should be reviewed from the perspective of the Rule of Sixths, which we first discussed in Chapter 7: About one-sixth of the agenda items should be from the past, what we used to call old business; about four-sixths, or two-thirds, should be from the "here and now"—current issues that are no older and no further in the future than one or two months.

The final sixth is the most important for entrepreneurial boards: These should be "blue sky" items—items of an anticipatory nature, looking ahead six months, a year, a year-and-a-half. These items represent the fun part of board meetings, when directors have the opportunity to look ahead, to influence the future, to structure their options. Here is where the Principle of Proactivity is really enforced. Although every meeting might not contain such items, most should because it allows for a certain amount of psychological rehearsal. Executives and other agenda schedulers have to anticipate the kinds of possibilities that may be coming up and take the board through a series of "what ifs." This not only permits the board to look ahead, it forces meeting planners, executives, and board chairs to look ahead and do a bit of scenario constructing.

It is amazing how beneficial this technique is. An advanced discussion of "what if" often permits the board to develop alternatives that no one has thought of before, introduces perspectives that previously have been concealed, and generally improves the quality of the eventual decision. Individual board chairs often tell us, "We don't have the time to do this." In our long experience with boards and the analysis of board decisions, this is just an excuse. Of course, emergencies occur from time to time, but if the board's whole life is a series of emergencies, then it is imperative that the board look at its decision-making system and try to anticipate issues and deal with them before they become emergencies.

The Rule of Three-Quarters

If the board is following the Rule of Halves, and the agenda scheduler receives all potential agenda items at the half-way point between meetings, then the Rule of Three-Quarters should be possible: An agenda with appropriate attachments should be distributed at the three-quarter point in time between meetings. For the board meeting monthly, that means three weeks after the last meeting and one week before the next.

Executives and other agenda schedulers usually have to work very hard during the "third quarter" between meetings. During this time, information necessary for the board to discuss agenda items is pulled together, presenters must be lined up, needed reports are copied, and so on. The Rule of Three-Quarters ensures that directors get information at just the right time before a meeting—not so late as to prevent them from reading it, and not so early as to invite them to put it aside.

This rule is one of the toughest to implement because lots of norms support handing out items at the meeting. Resist that temptation, get stuff out ahead of time, and expect people to read it!

The Rule of Two-Thirds

In the last chapter, we talked about the Three Characters Principle—all business in board meetings falls into one of three categories: announcements, decisions, and discussion. Following this principle, the Rule of Two-Thirds divides a meeting into three parts: The first third is the beginning or opening, where the announcements take place; the middle third is where the greatest amount of work is done, where the board makes decisions; the last third is a time for discussion and decompression. The two-thirds point is a good time for agenda schedulers to locate a break—a sort of seventh-inning stretch after the hard work is done and before winding down with discussion.

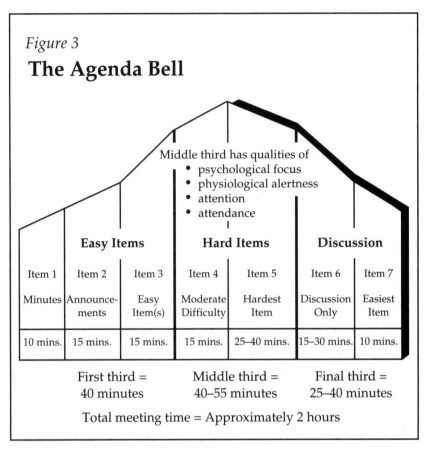

Figure 3

The Agenda Bell

Middle third has qualities of
- psychological focus
- physiological alertness
- attention
- attendance

	Easy Items		Hard Items		Discussion	
Item 1	Item 2	Item 3	Item 4	Item 5	Item 6	Item 7
Minutes	Announce-ments	Easy Item(s)	Moderate Difficulty	Hardest Item	Discussion Only	Easiest Item
10 mins.	15 mins.	15 mins.	15 mins.	25–40 mins.	15–30 mins.	10 mins.

First third =   Middle third =   Final third =
40 minutes   40–55 minutes   25–40 minutes

Total meeting time = Approximately 2 hours

The Rule of the Agenda Bell

Following the Principle of Three Characters and the Rule of
Two-Thirds, the agenda bell illustrates the ideal organization and flow of a board meeting. Assuming the agenda
scheduler has received all potential agenda items according
to the Rule of Halves, and has screened them using the Rule
of Sixths, the scheduler should outline all agenda items in
an ascending-descending order of difficulty, beginning the

meeting with relatively easy, noncontroversial items; building to the most difficult items in the middle of the meeting;
and tapering off to the easiest items, those for discussion,
at the end of the meeting.

With a seven-item agenda, the flow of the board meeting might look something like the agenda bell illustrated
in Figure 3 on page 173. Item 1 might be approval of the
minutes from the previous board meeting (assuming the
presence of a quorum) and should take no more than
10 minutes. Item 2 consists of a few brief, noncontroversial
announcements and should take no more than 15 minutes.
Item 3, of modest difficulty, typically lies within the first
portion of the meeting and begins the process of inviting
people to make decisions. The time for Item 3 is about 15
minutes, bringing the total time for the first third of the
meeting to 40 minutes.

The difficult decision items come in the middle third of
the meeting. Of modest difficulty, Item 4 may involve some
controversy, but not great controversy. Time: about 15 minutes. Item 5 is of the greatest difficulty and could take
25–40 minutes to complete. The most difficult items are
best scheduled to fall at the peak of the agenda bell. This is
the point by which most latecomers have arrived, early
leavers have not as yet slipped out. Attention, at this point,
is sharpest, and the psychological and physiological energy
necessary to deal with the complexities of the tough items
are highest.

Item 5 completes the first two-thirds of the meeting
agenda, which should take about 40–55 minutes total. This
is a good time to schedule that seventh-inning stretch. After
the break, the agenda shifts to discussion only and Item 6.
Items scheduled for this final third of the meeting do not
require decisions; issues can be discussed and thought

through. Item 6, which should involve 15–30 minutes of discussion, should allow the board to begin the process of deintensification and winding down, which is necessary for decision-making groups. The final item is always very easy and should take no more than 10 minutes to complete; its purpose is to put an end to the discussion in Item 6 and to end the meeting on a note of agreement (Item 7). Even though the agreement may be trivial, it is still important for group bonding. Total time for the final third of the meeting: 25–40 minutes.

Following the agenda bell, the entire meeting of seven items takes no more than 2 hours and 15 minutes. The agenda bell makes it possible to structure the meeting consonant with the flow of energy and within the time available for group decision making.

The Agenda Rule

The actual written agenda should be a clean, crisp document that is instructive and helpful. Its language reflects the decision and discussion aspects of the scheduled items, signaling directors in advance about each item's particular focus. The agenda should contain the following elements:

- The agenda is like a restaurant menu. The wording for each agenda item should be as specific as that for items on a menu. Avoid general wording. That would be like saying, "Meat," on a restaurant menu instead of "Roast Chicken."
- Following the menu concept, beneath each item write a brief statement concerning the essence of the item, just like restaurants do with their offerings.

- Beside each item, in parentheses, insert one of three character words: *action, discussion,* or *information.* Directors need to know the context of consideration as well as the actual substance.
- On the right-hand side of the "menu," in lieu of price, place a running clock, giving times for each item.

The sample agenda at right is organized according to the agenda bell.

The Rule of Reports

Most reports are too long and do not contain the essential information necessary for quality decisions. The Rule of Reports argues for an executive summary-type of report— an options memo—divided into three parts:

- a statement of the problem;
- a list of possible solutions;
- an outline of which option seems most reasonable and is recommended by the person or committee preparing the report.

This three-part executive summary-style of report is not only briefer than the typical long report, but it also gives the board some tools with which to work. Placing the recommended solution following the other options allows decision makers to consider options previously unrecognized, possibly combine them with the recommended option, and come up with a stronger, better-quality decision. Although the reporting individual or group may strongly support the recommended solution, they should resist any temptation to eliminate options other than the

Board Meeting Agenda

Call to Order	*7:00 P.M.*
1. Minutes (Action)	*7:00–7:10*
2. Announcements (Information)	*7:10–7:25*

    a. Holiday schedules for staff
    b. Holiday open house needs board members
       present throughout the day.
    c. Installation of new smoke alarms.
    d. Other matters

3. Approval of Grant Submission to Youth
   Services (Action)   *7:25–7:40*
   Money to support discharged youth is requested
   from Youth Services Bureau. (Program Committee)

4. Mileage Rebate Change (Action)   *7:40–7:55*
   We wish to increase the mileage allowance from
   18¢ to 24¢ per mile. (Finance Committee)

5. Board Training (Action)   *7:55–8:35*
   A day-long plan for board training is proposed.
   A copy of the proposal is attached.
   (Training Committee)

6. Board Manual (Discussion)   *8:35–8:55*
   Should we have a directors' manual? What should
   it contain? A preliminary outline, for discussion
   only, is attached. (Training Committee)

7. Approval of Official Letter of Thanks to Della
   Furlong (Action)   *8:55–9:00*
   Ms. Furlong reached her 25th anniversary with
   the agency this year.

Adjourn	*9:00 P.M.*

recommendation. Removing the options takes away from the decision-making group one of its most powerful tools and creates a rubber-stamp situation for the recommendations.

A sample options memo appears at right.

The Rule of Minutes

The Rule of Minutes calls for agenda-relevant content minutes rather than process minutes. Content minutes outline each topic on the agenda, provide a brief summary of the issue and the various points of view, and then, in different type, state the decision. Done properly, content minutes can handle most issues in a paragraph or two. Directors will find this system more comprehensible and intelligible than other systems of minute-taking, especially process minutes, which have endless streams of "he said" or "she said."

Agenda relevance simply means that the numbering system in the minutes should parallel that of the agenda, making it easy for readers to find the minutes in reference to particular items. This system prevents the minutes from simply rehashing last month's meeting. Sample minutes prepared according to this rule appear on page 180.

The Rule of Agenda Integrity

To maintain agenda integrity, the chair, directors, executive, and agency staff must ensure that all items on the agenda are discussed and that items not on the agenda are not discussed. If directors are expected to invest their time reading materials in preparation for the meetings,

Options Memo

Memorandum

To: Board of Directors, ChildHelp America

From: Training Committee

Re: Board Training Proposal

The Problem

The Children's Center is more than 30 years old. A recent visit from our outside consulting firm has raised some serious questions about the vigor and responsibility of the board. The consultant's report suggested that the board has let the executive take too much initiative and that the board needs "invigoration," to use the consultant's phrase. The matter was turned over to the Executive Committee, which created a Training Committee to make a proposal to the board.

Options

We have several directions to consider:

- doing nothing, in spite of the criticism;
- beginning a planned improvement of board activity and involvement in decision making—a one-day training session;
- working to improve selected areas of board activity.

Recommendation

The committee recommends Option 2. We feel that doing nothing is not acceptable, and if one group raises this question, others cannot be far behind. Too, the executive feels that a bit more is needed than just an overall program of board improvement, and that piecemeal activities should be part of that overall plan. We recognize that several directors feel this is a waste of time, but hope that discussion of this proposal will lead to its approval. The committee has some ideas about the possible content of the day-long training session, once the board gives its approval in principle.

Sample Board Minutes

Board Minutes

1. **Previous Minutes**

   Minutes of the last meeting were approved as submitted.

2. **Announcements**

   a. Staff holiday schedules were announced.

   b. The board was reminded that the Holiday Open House needs members present throughout the day.

   c. New smoke alarms are being installed.

3. **Grant to Youth Services Board**

   The board approved submission of an $8,000 grant request to the Youth Services Board for follow-up studies. One director was reluctant, noting that too much time was going into research.

4. **Mileage Rate**

   The Finance Committee's proposal to increase mileage reimbursement from 18¢ to 24¢ was modified. The board approved a rate of 20¢ this year, 22¢ for next year, and 24¢ for the following year.

5. **Board Training Plan**

   Board training plan was approved in principle. There was considerable discussion of the idea of board "training." Several directors took exception to that language. Two directors abstained. The Training Committee was instructed to prepare a day-long schedule for final approval.

6. **Discussion of Directors' Manual**

   There was considerable discussion of the Directors' Manual. Directors felt the outline was helpful and will provide suggestions to the Training Committee by October 1.

7. **Letter of Thanks**

   An official letter of appreciation to Della Furlong, acknowledging her 25th anniversary with the agency, was approved and signed by all directors.

then that investment must pay off in the discussion within the meeting. When issues on the agenda, and for which directors have prepared, are not discussed in the meeting, or when items not on the agenda, and for which directors have not been allowed to prepare, are interjected into the meeting, directors conclude that preparation is not a good investment of their time, and they start avoiding the task altogether.

The Rule of Temporal Integrity

Temporal integrity means to watch the clock. Begin the meeting on time, end on time, and follow the rough time estimates suggested by the agenda bell.

Posting times next to the items on the agenda, as suggested by the Agenda Rule, is helpful because it gives people a rough idea of how long the agenda scheduler feels is appro-priate to spend on each particular item. This rule is especially important for minor items that tend to balloon and take inordinate amounts of time. The sample agenda on page 177 uses this system. By starting with more modest items—minutes and announcements—if people are a bit late, not a great deal is lost.

Starting on time is the best way to get people to come on time; and the meeting should always end on time, even if it gets to a bit of a late start. Ending board meetings on time is crucial.

Planning Sets the Stage

These rules involve setting the stage for the meeting. The kind of meeting planning we discuss here makes it possible to complete the board's business within allotted times. The dynamic aspect of board meetings—role playing and using decision rules—requires attention as well. These topics are covered in the next chapter.

Chapter 17

Three Key Roles for Effective Board Meetings

We have previously discussed the overall roles of the chair, the individual director, and the executive. We examine here the specific roles that these three positions play in the board meeting itself. As the saying goes, this is where the rubber hits the road, especially for board chairs and directors.

The Chair

The chairperson must assume a stance in board meetings that considers the range of alternatives and does not argue against individuals within the group. Indeed, the chair supports both individual directors in their sharing of ideas and the ideas themselves. Even if a director's idea is not the greatest, it may inspire someone else to suggest just what is needed.

The chair models behavior for members. If the chair attacks a proposal, then others are sure to follow. Instead, the chair should demonstrate through behavior, courtesy, attentive listening, and interest.

Nor does the chair advance pet ideas. That is not leadership. Rather, the chair promotes a blending of others' ideas, putting together components from the ideas of several people. The chair provides vision and overall direction, but it is not appropriate for the chair to use the role as a vehicle for implementing one's own ideas.

Part of the chair's role is to facilitate the accomplishment of assigned tasks by all members of the group. The chair should not be a jack- (or "Jacquelyn") of-all-trades, trying to do it all himself or herself; that's not the appropriate role of the chair. If the chairperson is doing everything, then he or she has to start working on delegation skills.

Part of the chair's role also involves overseeing the preparation and organization of the physical meeting space, being sure that tables and chairs are in their proper order, cleaning up after groups that have not been so courteous, and leaving the meeting room in such a condition that others can use it after the meeting ends. This is a difficult and onerous task, and one that many directors often pass to clerical staff and others. But the chair doesn't have to do all this alone. Recruiting staff members and other directors in this task is appropriate; this kind of involvement is precisely what the chair should seek to accomplish. But it is the chair's responsibility to see that these tasks are completed. That's what we mean by *delegation*.

The chair also acts as an administrator in working with the executive to ensure that all necessary materials for the meeting are ready and available and, following the Rule of Three-Quarters, are sent to the directors under the appropriate time guidelines. Although an agenda scheduler may be assigned this task, the chair is ultimately responsible for ensuring that the task is completed. The chair has no business complaining that directors don't come prepared for the meetings if the chair doesn't see to it that the appropriate materials go out on time.

When the meeting starts, the chair has to be prepared for the issues under discussion as well as the attitudes, values, and points of view of the individual directors. The Rule of Halves, and the discussion that occurs while putting the agenda together under the Rule of Halves, helps the chair to prepare for the meeting in this way. Sometimes, as we discuss later in this chapter, the executive director helps prepare the chairperson by briefing her or him on what individual directors think and what their positions might be on particular issues. This kind of information is important and appropriate for the chair to have. Walking into a meeting without it leaves the chair open to criticism.

The chair has to be balanced. For example, the chair's presentation of an issue must clearly take into account all sides. Slighting one side, making snide remarks, or using body language to convey disagreement with a particular position is not acceptable behavior. Similar constraints apply to relationships with the public at large and the media.

As the meeting progresses, the chair tries to ensure that all directors have equal access to the floor. All groups have members who are eager to participate and those who are shy or reluctant to participate. To get the full range of views on the floor, however, the chair must control the overparticipator and encourage the underparticipator. Those who are slighted by the more aggressive participants in the meeting are frequently among those who complain after the meeting.

As we discuss in some detail in the next chapter, the chair must take the lead in summarizing and crystallizing issues for action. If the chair does not take leadership in decision, summary, and crystallization, the board simply spins its wheels, going round and round on the same issue.

Finally, the chair should follow *Robert's Rules of Order* or some other form of orderly procedure that facilitates decision making. There is no magic in *Robert's Rules of Order*. Indeed, Henry M. Robert was an Army officer, so his views on how meetings should run may be overly formal. What is important is that the chair follow some set of rules to maintain order and keep the meeting running smoothly.[1] The "play it by ear" approach often slights people and can leave a lot of resentment.

The Director

The director's responsibilities mirror those of the chair in many ways. First, the director must come to meetings well-prepared and must encourage others to do the same. The second half of this responsibility may seem a bit odd to some directors. Good examples are the social legitimacy of asking the passengers in one's car to use their seat belts, or the new acceptability of asking one's guests not to smoke. It used to be very intemperate to say anything, regardless of the one's own feelings. Today, however, it is quite acceptable to ask, "Excuse me, but would you mind putting on your seat belt?" or "Would you mind terribly not smoking in the house?" That one's colleagues on the board come to meetings prepared is a similarly legitimate expectation. Asking others to undertake certain responsi-

---

[1]   The League of Women Voters has developed a pamphlet containing a quick, informal set of rules that are useful for board meetings. See League of Women Voters. (1979). *Simplified parliamentary procedure.* [Pamphlet]. Washington, DC: Author.

bilities should be encouraged within meetings. If a director is making comments on material that he or she has clearly not read, it should be legitimate to ask that person to look at the material.

Directors should take initiative to participate in the board's discussions. The "Silent Sam" or "Quiet Kate" technique is rapidly falling out of favor with directors. Certainly, some people are shier than others and find it more difficult to participate in groups than do others. Individuals should not leave it up to the chair, however, to always ask them to participate. Rather, each director should take that initiative and join in the discussions, at least often enough so that he or she doesn't become known as "that quiet person."

Conversely, directors should temper any tendency to overparticipate, instead matching the amount of their participation to that of their colleagues in the group. Obviously, this may not always be the case. On some issues, one will feel more exercised and passionate than with others. Rather, directors should be alert to patterns of over- or underparticipation.

Directors should also be alert to those issues that occur outside the board's framework but would be of interest to the board, and bring them to the board's attention. Each member is part of the board's intelligence network. Sometimes, this involves simply alerting the board about items in the local press on issues of interest to the board. Other times, it involves reporting conversations and the like. Directors should contribute proactively to the board's intelligence system.

Directors should follow through with assignments and requests for work. In Chapter 13, we talked about evaluating individual directors, and part of this evaluation takes into account whether directors are indeed following through. Of course, people forget and get sidetracked. The Rule of Halves, however, enables the chairperson or the executive director to remind directors about agreed-upon responsibilities. Directors, collectively with the chair, try to ensure a fair division of labor in which everyone chips in.

Finally, directors refrain from criticizing the board to others outside the boardroom. The director is a member of the group, even if a decision made by the group is one with which the director disagrees. To share those disappointments with others is a violation of basic ethical norms.

The Executive Director

With the board chair, the executive director is responsible for the mechanical and substantive functioning of the board meeting and for meetings of board committees. As a practical matter, and as the only regularly paid participant at the board meeting, the executive director usually is the person who "puts it all together."

Typically, the executive director is an ex officio director and, as such, has the right to participate as a full director but does not have a vote. When the executive director works with the board in this way, it is often called "staffing" the board.

On the mechanical side, the executive director often plays the role of agenda scheduler, as discussed in Chapter 16. That involves getting the items for the meeting from relevant parties and organizing them (using the Rule of the Agenda Bell) for the upcoming meeting. Also involved here is the organization of any reports. Following the Rule of Three-Quarters, the executive director sends out materials for the next monthly meeting about one week before the meeting is scheduled.

The executive director provides or supervises vital editorial support and recordkeeping by documenting the proceedings of board meetings and taking notes that are later transcribed into minutes. Working with the chair, the executive director also prepares communications from the board to other organizations, such as letters, drafts, reports, and memos.

The executive director also acts as a researcher, gathering information at the board's request from libraries, books, journals, memos, minutes, and other organizations to help the board carry out its function. The executive director compiles and interprets research data, offering recommendations as to how it applies to the particular area of investigation. This is what happens when the executive director prepares a report to the board under the Rule of Reports. It does not do the board much good to simply collect a bunch of information and dump it, via the copy machine, on the directors. Rather, the executive director needs to collate, compile, organize, and process the information so that directors receive a comprehensible, intelligible report on the research. This report typically includes a statement of the problem, options, and recommendations, as indicated in the Rule of Reports.

This function of gathering and compiling data and making recommendations raises an important point. To make quality decisions, the board needs all appropriate information on a particular issue, as well as a full outline of the available options. Sometimes, that information and those options may run counter to the executive director's own views; but, as a professional, the executive director must be able to set aside his or her own views when they differ with the data or the recommendations. The professional is assessing a situation and bringing the news to the board for discussion and review—just as an attorney, for example, will bring precedents to the attention of a client, even if they do not support that client's case, so that the client may consider them.

Similarly, the executive director should participate only moderately in board discussions. Boards frequently give up their deliberations too easily and too quickly, turning to the executive director and saying, "Let's just do what the pros think." As tempting as it might be for the executive director to share his or her professional views strongly, our advice is to approach the situation in a balanced fashion. Board decision making is not always enhanced when professionals take over and give their views.

The executive director recognizes and points out ambiguous data to the board. Not all data will fall into neat piles of pros and cons. Indeed, data may be unavailable or of dubious quality, and the board must rely on the executive director to point out what is certain and what is less than certain. Obviously, the directors and board chair will make some of these judgments on their own, but they are guided by the executive director's professionalism in these considerations.

If the executive director has been in place for some time, he or she can be a great resource in terms of institutional memory. Directors and board chairs come and go, but the executive director may know the history of an issue and the trajectory of approaches toward a particular problem, both within the agency itself and among others. Simply getting information from the library, though important, is not always sufficient. There may be programmatic lore and culture that bear upon the board's consideration of an issue within this particular agency context. A Jewish agency, a Catholic agency, an African American agency, a Latino agency may each have its own particular view on certain matters, and these should be brought to the board's attention as it considers the issue or problem. Similarly, the executive director may offer a political assessment as well. Knowing how powerful people feel about the issues in question can be very helpful to the board. What is the political lay of the land? Although such analyses may not always make a difference, sometimes they may be very important to the board's deliberations.

"Across the Board" Application

This discussion of the dynamics of board meetings and the roles of the chair, director, and executive director applies, as well, to meetings within the board's committee structure and within the agency itself. Performing these roles is immensely complex. In fact, proper *role* performance is more difficult and complex than proper *rule* performance. Rule performance is methodical and mechanical: The Rule of Halves, the Rules of Sixths, and so on, do not involve great difficulties in implementation, although they may involve a certain amount of discipline. Once one gets into role performance, however, one's life is immediately filled with complexity and nuance. In implementing these role prescriptions, therefore, one should expect a certain amount of uncertainty at first. Only in time will the roles become smooth, seamless, and, ultimately, flawless.

No set of rules can guarantee perfect meetings; directors with a lot of meeting experience certainly know this. It's also true, however, that, for many reasons—lack of training and lack of preparation, especially—we tend to approach board meetings casually and with a relaxed sense of mission. To a certain extent, of course, this is good. One should not take these things too seriously. On the other hand, considering the important range of activities for which directors are responsible and the potential legal liabilities that they may suffer if they do their job poorly, a systematic and planful approach to decision making is certainly a good place to start.

As the central vehicle through which effective directorship takes place, the board meeting is the crucial tool. There are simple ways—outlined in Chapters 15–17—to make board meetings a source of surprise and delight. Evaluation is a key step, and the following exercise is customized to the material in these chapters to facilitate such assessment.

Exercise 14

Now that we have discussed the principles, rules, and roles necessary for effective board meetings, as well as how to analyze the board's decision making, we offer here a model for assessing your meetings to determine the strengths and weaknesses in your board's decision-making process.[2] Your board can use the feedback obtained here to improve its effectiveness. Boards should conduct this evaluation periodically—we recommend every six months.

Any committee member or board director can use this instrument; chairs can make especially good use of it.

The model should enable the group to examine its method of conducting meetings; that analysis, in turn, can provide information to help the group change and improve

---

[2] University of Michigan student Stannett Amy contributed to the development of this assessment instrument.

its performance. Unless the board analyzes the results of this evaluation, however, and implements recommendations based on these results, the effort here will be wasted.

Instructions

The evaluator should begin by observing five meetings of the board or committee being assessed. After five meetings, the evaluator completes the assessment form, indicating at how many of the meetings each rule was followed or task accomplished.[3]

In evaluating directors or committee members, the evaluator may, upon the board's recommendation, apply the questions to each individual member of the group, or rate the membership as a whole. In the latter case, rather than answer "Yes" or "No" for each item, the evaluator should use three response categories: None to One-Third (in compliance), One-Third to Two-Thirds, and Two-Thirds to All.

Responses to individual items can be scored as percentages. For example, tasks completed in one meeting out of five would receive a 20% score; in two meetings, 40%; three meetings, 60%; and so on. Similarly, answers regarding board roles, individually or collectively, can be averaged to obtain percentage scores.

The evaluator can use the instrument as a discussion guide, involving all members of the group in the assessment.

---

[3]   Five meetings may be a lot. Feel free to customize this form for as few as two meetings, or even one.

Assessing Board Meetings

Out of five meetings observed, in how many was each rule followed or each task completed?

	0	1	2	3	4	5

Agenda Scheduling Rules

Rule of Halves

0	1	2	3	4	5
❑	❑	❑	❑	❑	❑

Items for next meeting must be in the hands of the agenda scheduler one-half of time between meetings.

Rule of Sixths

0	1	2	3	4	5
❑	❑	❑	❑	❑	❑

One-sixth of agenda items relate to past issues; one-sixth are future issues. Remaining four-sixths are current issues.

Rule of Three-Quarters

0	1	2	3	4	5
❑	❑	❑	❑	❑	❑

Agenda scheduler sends out packets of material for next meeting at the three-quarter point between meetings.

Rule of Two-Thirds

0	1	2	3	4	5
❑	❑	❑	❑	❑	❑

Meeting divided into three parts: start-up period (announcements), period of heavy work (decisions), and period of discussion and decompression.

Assessing Board Meetings (continued)

Out of five meetings observed, in how many was each rule followed or each task completed?

	0	1	2	3	4	5

Agenda Bell Rule

Item 1, Minutes
Simple, straightforward.
Read and ratified (if quorum
is present).

| | ❑ | ❑ | ❑ | ❑ | ❑ | ❑ |

Item 2, Announcements
Brief, noncontroversial,
few in number.

| | ❑ | ❑ | ❑ | ❑ | ❑ | ❑ |

Item 3, Easy Item(s)
Items need action, decision
but are relatively
noncontroversial.

| | ❑ | ❑ | ❑ | ❑ | ❑ | ❑ |

Item 4, Moderate Difficulty
Items potentially
controversial, fairly complex.

| | ❑ | ❑ | ❑ | ❑ | ❑ | ❑ |

Item 5, Hardest Item(s)
Major decisions, highly
controversial and complex.

| | ❑ | ❑ | ❑ | ❑ | ❑ | ❑ |

Break
Seventh-inning stretch

| | ❑ | ❑ | ❑ | ❑ | ❑ | ❑ |

Item 6, Discussion Item(s)
Discussion only of items to be
decided at future meetings.

| | ❑ | ❑ | ❑ | ❑ | ❑ | ❑ |

Item 7, Easiest Item(s)
Small decisions of no great
importance that serve to unify
the group.

| | ❑ | ❑ | ❑ | ❑ | ❑ | ❑ |

Assessing Board Meetings (continued)

Out of five meetings observed, in how many was each rule followed or each task completed?

	0	1	2	3	4	5

Meeting Rules

Agenda Rule ❑ ❑ ❑ ❑ ❑ ❑
Agenda written in inviting, clear manner. One-sentence summary and estimated time follows each agenda item.

Rule of Reports ❑ ❑ ❑ ❑ ❑ ❑
Executive summaries and option memos are primary sources for decision making within meeting.

Rule of Minutes ❑ ❑ ❑ ❑ ❑ ❑
Minutes correspond to agenda, are content-relevant, and focus on decisions.

Agenda Integrity Rule ❑ ❑ ❑ ❑ ❑ ❑
All items on agenda are discussed. Items not on agenda are not discussed.

Temporal Integrity Rule ❑ ❑ ❑ ❑ ❑ ❑
Meeting begins and ends on time and generally adheres to projected time estimates for agenda items.

Assessing Board Roles

The Chair	% of Time in 5 Meetings	Comments
Leads group to consider alternatives. Supports directors both in sharing of ideas and in ideas themselves.		
Models appropriate board behavior to other members of the group.		
Works to synthesize ideas rather than promote pet ideas and projects.		
Facilitates task accomplishment by all members of group rather than doing it all him- or herself.		
Acts administratively to see that meeting area is prepared for meeting and cleaned afterward and that all required materials are ready and available.		
Researches both issues and attitudes of directors in preparation for meeting.		
Presents balanced representation of the board to the outside, avoiding one-sided, intemperate statements to the public and the media.		

Assessing Board Roles (continued)

The Chair *(cont.)*	% of Time in 5 Meetings	Comments
Ensures all directors have equal opportunity to be heard on any issue.		
Allows more time during meeting for large issues, less time for smaller issues.		
Summarizes, crystallizes, and focuses discussion once everyone has a chance to speak on an issue.		
Follows *Robert's Rules of Order* or some other orderly procedure.		
The Executive Director	% of Time in 5 Meetings	Comments
Acts as researcher, gathering information at board's request.		
Compiles and interprets researched data; makes recommendations as to how data apply to issues before board.		
Recognizes and points out ambiguous data to board.		
Includes necessary, appropriate information, even if it runs counter to his or her own views.		
Refrains from presenting slanted or purposefully unclear views to board.		

The Executive Director (cont.)	% of Time in 5 Meetings	Comments
Presents written documentation but avoids influencing discussion. Participates in discussion professionally.		
Source of institutional history—how board has handled similar issues in the past, how organization differs today from when previous decisions were made, etc.		
Source of political information—such as views of those in positions of power within and outside the organization and in government.		
Sees that proceedings are documented.		
Prepares communications from board on request.		
Working with chair, prepares drafts of memos and reports for board review and revision.		
Assists chair when necessary to ensure meeting requirements are met, meeting space is prepared, and cleanup and follow-through are accomplished.		

Assessing Board Roles *(continued)*

The Executive Director *(cont.)*	% of Time in 5 Meetings	Comments
Checks potential agenda items at halfway point between meetings.		
Makes sure directors receive agenda by three-quarters point between meetings.		
Confirms day, date, time, and location of meeting with directors, making necessary adjustments to accommodate special individual and group needs.		
Individual Director, Committee Member	% of Time in 5 Meetings	Comments
Comes to meetings well-prepared, encourages others to do same.		
Participates without prodding to take part in discussions.		
Tempers tendency to overparticipate.		
Overall participation about the same as that of other group members.		
Alert to and pursues outside information and perspectives that may be of use to the board.		
Follows through with assignments and requests.		

Individual Director (cont.)	% of Time in 5 Meetings	Comments
Portrays board as decision-making body rather than a group of individuals; speaks of board decisions or policies, not internal dissent.		

Directors, Committee Members as a Group	0–1/3 of group	1/3–2/3 of group	2/3–All of group
Come to meetings well-prepared, encourage others to do same.	❏	❏	❏
Participate without prodding to take part in discussions.	❏	❏	❏
Temper tendency to overparticipate.	❏	❏	❏
Overall participation about the same as rest of group.	❏	❏	❏
Alert to and pursue outside information and perspectives that may be of use to board.	❏	❏	❏
Follow through with assignments and requests.	❏	❏	❏
Portray board as decision-making body rather than group of individuals; speak of board decisions or policies, not internal dissent.	❏	❏	❏

Comments

Summary

What things are we doing well that should be continued?

What are we doing less well that should phased out or stopped?

What are we not now doing but should begin?

Comments

Chapter 18

Decision Rules and Decision Crystallization

How are decisions actually made in boards—or in meetings anywhere, for that matter? The obvious answer might be "consensus." But defining *consensus* is a daunting task.

Our research suggests that decisions are made on the basis of decision rules. Decision rules are norms that make decisions legitimate. There are at least five decision rules used by groups in any given meeting. Each rule is one we all know and believe in. Each conflicts and competes with the others, in the sense that using any one individually would advance certain interests and ignore others. They must be used in concert. Appreciation and management of decision rules is one of the largest—but largely unacknowledged—jobs of boards.

Five Major Decision Rules

The breadth decision rule, or the voting rule, is the one most commonly used by boards of directors in their public actions and is frequently written into organization bylaws. This rule, which has a long tradition in North American society, states that each person has a single vote.

Important as this rule is, however, it fails to take into account other important interests. For example, the breadth decision rule deals with neither the intensity of one's opinions on a decision matter, nor the level of one's involvement in particular matters under consideration. Thus, other decision rules come into play, often informally.

The intensity decision rule gives weight to those who feel strongly about an issue. Boards that use this rule usually try to probe for depth of feeling among their voting members. It protects minority interests. If you were the only vegetarian in a group, you might never call for a vote on the dinner menu if you knew you were going to be outvoted by the nonvegetarians every time.

The involvement decision rule considers the preferences of those who might have to carry out a decision. If the board is voting on a particular action that an individual director has to carry out, that director is much more involved and may have a greater interest in the outcome than her or his colleagues. After all, they don't have to do it. Thus, the involvement decision rule gives weight to those with greater involvement. Frequently in board meetings, when someone says something like, "I'd like to hear what Sheila has to say because, after all, she has to do it," the involvement decision rule is being applied. This rule gives the executive director great influence, since he or she is often the one who carries out board policies.

The expert decision rule takes account of one's specialized knowledge in a particular issue before the board. Some people know more than others. Attorneys on boards, for example, frequently receive great respect when legal matters come up. Similarly, boards often defer to physicians when medical matters come up. Boards often take into strong account one's expertise in a particular area of decision making when an issue reaches a vote.

The power decision rule. None of these rules deal with social or political power and influence. That is where the power decision rule comes in. Corporations frequently phrase this decision rule as: "What does the boss want?" This rule gives individuals of high organizational authority—the board chair or the executive director, for example—greater weight. It also gives people of great social status, such as physicians or attorneys, influence beyond their technical expertise that extends into matters of which they have no greater knowledge than anyone else. The board listens to and heeds them, however, because of their social power.

Managing Decision Rules

These five rules operate simultaneously in boards. Though the board may take formal votes, the votes frequently come only after the directors have considered the decision from the perspectives of the other four rules. Directors and chairs should be aware of the competition among the rules and the fact that different rules may have greater weight under different conditions.

They must also remember that the rules are not neutral. Individual directors may often advocate certain decision rules that, overall, favor their interests. For example, if a particular director favors a proposal and believes that she or he has the votes necessary for passage, very likely that director will advocate, "Let's just take a vote." On the other hand, if the director does not appear to have the votes, she or he may advocate other decision rules, such as listening to those who are better informed or who are more involved in the issue.

Generally speaking, the alert chair should invoke at least two decision rules in proposing that the decision go forward. This is especially true in the action or decision hypothesis stage of decision crystallization, which we discuss later in this chapter. Consider, for example, the statement, "Most of us seem to favor the course of action under discussion [breadth rule], and that action meets the needs of those who are most knowledgeable [expert rule] and most involved [involvement rule]."

Directors may not have thought of the decision making in quite this way before. This awareness can lead to a more detailed and in-depth understanding of what is actually transpiring when alternatives are proposed and either accepted or rejected. Invoking two or more decision rules in a particular instance enhances the likelihood of a successful decision.

The Decision Mosaic

Most of what we think of as decisions really comprise smaller decision elements that are assembled in a *decision mosaic*. Consider a simple board decision, such as whether to have a board retreat. One might expect the issue to require only a simple yes or no vote. In fact, however, the decision represents a composite of smaller decisions— about time and location, about the facilitator, about who should organize it, and so on. Each of these is a decision element. Effective board chairs facilitate and lead the development of an overall decision mosaic. They build the decision, so to speak, element by element, until the mosaic is assembled. Then, the chair helps the group engage in *decision sculpting*, in which the overall decision is examined and its elements adjusted to create a higher-quality decision.

The job of the board chair, therefore, is to identify the elements to be considered in the decision mosaic. Simply put, that means breaking the decision into reasonable elements that the group can consider. Without this step, a typical scenario develops, in which the chair asks, "What should we discuss at the board retreat?" From around the table come individual shouts of, "Programs," "Let's have good food," "How about meeting at a nice location?" and "Let's eat earlier than last year." Each contribution is important and appropriate by itself. Unfortunately, since one does not follow from the other, the decision-building process is very difficult. Instead, the chair should identify the initial topic to discuss—perhaps the retreat program—and then proceed, element by element, to build a mosaic.

Decision building occurs via rounds of discussion in which each director who so desires has a chance to offer one opinion once. When the chair asks, "Anyone else have a view?" and no additional views are forthcoming, it's time for the chair to begin the process of *decision crystallization* for that particular decision element. The chair does not have to be the only person who undertakes decision crystallization, but unless the chair models both the procedure and the willingness to undertake the risk of rejection involved in proposing action, no one else will be willing to undertake it.

Decision crystallization is a four-part process. The first step is *summative reflection.* At the end of a round of discussion, the chair, who has been listening to and pulling together the different elements of the discussion, summarizes for the group what has been said. Groups do not actually know what individual group members think until the members have had a chance to share their views. A neutral, factual pulling together of the views expressed in the group is the first step towards decision crystallization. For example, the chair might say, "Okay, what I'm hearing is a general agreement that a training retreat for the board is a good idea. There are some concerns about scheduling the retreat around other agency events, and some opposition to the notion that directors who have served on the board for some time should have to go through 'training.' Two good sites for the retreat have been suggested."

The second step is the *decision suggestion* or *action hypothesis*. Based on the views expressed in the summary, the chair risks suggesting action: "I suggest that the board start planning a directors' retreat to be held in July at North Lake State Park, after the agency's anniversary celebration. The content of the retreat should take into account that the board has several experienced directors as well as a number of new directors."

It is extremely important that action or decision be suggested at this juncture. Groups often do not know whether they want to do something until someone actually makes a proposal. A familiar example is the age-old question, "Where should we go to dinner tonight?" Often, colleagues or family members say, "Gee, I don't know," or "It doesn't matter to me," until someone suggests, "Let's have Chinese." At that point, under the threat of action, preferences become highlighted. Thus, decisions and actions offered in the decision suggestion or action hypotheses stage are frequently rejected: "July's not a good time," "What about a local hotel instead of the state park?" "I'm still concerned• about the content." That's fine; it's supposed to be that way. It's one way in which the group explores what it does and does not want. Over time, of course, as the chair becomes more skilled at understanding the underlying commonalties and uniformities of group life, the proposed action or decision will be more on the mark. Some people always seem to get their suggestions accepted. One wonders what special skills they possess. Frequently, they simply listen carefully and extract the common themes from among ostensibly diverse suggestions.

The third step, *legitimization,* follows directly from decision suggestion and provides for the board the reasons why the proposal is okay. These reasons articulate the decision rules. So, the chairperson might summarize views about the retreat and then say, "It seems that a retreat is a good idea [the decision suggestion is vocalized] because [here comes the legitimization] most of us think it is okay [breadth rule] and there is no strong opposition [intensity rule]. Sheila, who has to much of the planning, thinks it's fine [involvement rule], and Tropman and Tropman recommend it [expert rule]. Looks like the retreat's a go!"

Let's assume for a moment that, with nods and murmurs of agreement, the group members signal their acceptance of the chair's decision suggestion. At this point, the chair moves to the fourth stage, *discussion refocus.* Once the group reaches a tentative agreement on one element, the chair directs the group toward the next element up for discussion, targeting the group's attention and discussion and avoiding divergent, digressing, or conflicting topics.

Board decision making thus proceeds, element by element, building to the final mosaic. When the group has assembled all the pieces of a particular decision mosaic, and all of the relevant elements have been tentatively decided, the chair then invites the group to step back and look at the total package. Do all of the elements fit together in a synchronous and harmonious way? Should the board adjust earlier decisions in the mosaic because of the nature of later decisions. If, for example, in decorating an office, it turns out that inadvertently all of the colors chosen were beige, then one might wish to modify some of the colors. This question is difficult to approach, however, until the directors have reviewed all the elements of the decision. This overall review is called *decision sculpting.*

Suppose, however, that in the decision suggestion stage, a proposed direction is not accepted. That is, indeed, a very likely result. At that juncture, the chair should back off from the offering or proposal. The original purpose of the suggestion was not to ensure acceptance of that particular direction, but rather to help the group in its discussion and consideration of the decision. So if someone turns out to have a negative view about holding the retreat in our example—some issue or question that is now known because its possibility has been stated—then the chair proposes another round of discussion but seeks to ratchet down the alternatives in a couple of ways.

One way would be for the chair to remove the option of a retreat from the table. A second way might be to propose some other minor options for the board's consideration—such as holding longer meetings or a series of special meetings—as well as new ideas. Thus, the next round of discussion on the same element occurs with a reduced and refocused number of alternatives. The board can go through two or three rounds of discussion, each time narrowing and refocusing until it achieves a tentative decision on an element in the mosaic.

This process of decision crystallization is one of the central aids to high-quality decision making in boards. Where it occurs, decisions are likely to be viable and reflective of a range of input. Where it is not used, decisions are likely to be haphazard, "by guess and by gosh," and very lucky to be on the mark. Although board decision making certainly has creative aspects, which should not be set aside, it also has very focused, very deliberate, almost mechanical procedures, which, if used, can be of great help to the group. Indeed, as in many other areas of life—such as driving or perfecting one's golf swing or tennis serve—the initial rules will eventually fade from consciousness and the group will proceed through them almost automatically.

The focus, so far, has been on the chairperson as the decision crystallizer. Indeed, as we noted above, if the chair models this behavior, others will pick it up. Sometimes, however, a situation arises in which the chair must reverse the procedure and decrystallize a decision, which we first discussed in Chapter 12. Typically, boards have difficulty reaching quality decisions in a timely manner. Hence, the emphasis in board deliberations is often on decision facilitation. Boards sometimes come to decisions too quickly, without a thoughtful, reflective approach to the subject matter. Sometimes, as we discussed in Chapter 7, decisions may be conservative or overboard and, thus, of questionable quality. In this event, the chair or others might interrupt the decision crystallization process. This involves broadening rather than narrowing the field of alternatives for consideration. In the case of premature closure, for example, when a board comes together and quickly says, "Let's do this," decrystallization introduces a range of other alternatives and raises questions about the implications and potential costs of those alternatives. Hopefully, these interventions create enough uncertainty within some members of the group to move agreement from a critical mass to a marginal mass, and then open the entire subject for more detailed, thoughtful consideration.

Agenda item preparation and agenda timing are extremely important to decision crystallization. That is the primary reason for the Rule of Halves in Chapter 16. If the board does not have adequate time to consider issues, then it will likely be forced either into making a decision too quickly or toward conservative, "Let's do it as we've done" procedures and decisions. Providing enough time to consider issues is an important first step toward changing and improving the board.

Why Decisions Fail

Quality board decision making depends on several factors: being aware of the backgrounds of individual directors and staff, following the correct rules and procedures for group meetings, and understanding the dynamics and roles in the decision process. Group members and chairs need an additional perspective, however, that focuses on the decision rules. This little known but very important element of group decision making can make or break the board's decision strategy.

The decision-making process is deeply complex and involves not only substance, but rules. Outstanding proposals often do not get the support necessary for their implementation because chairs and other directors fail to understand the need to consider expertise, power, depth of involvement, and extensiveness of involvement at the point at which the decision is made. Board deliberations can often reach a stalemate when group members invoke competing rules, and chairs and directors do not know how to proceed. The likelihood of high-quality board decisions is greatly enhanced when directors are aware of, understand, and follow these decision rules.

Exercise 15

Which decision rules does your board use, and how often (in percentage of time)? On a scale of 1 to 5 (1 being the highest and 5 being the lowest), what weight does your board place on each rule?

Rules	Use	Frequency	Weights
Breadth Decision Rule (Voting Rule)			
Intensity Decision Rule			
Involvement Decision Rule			
Expert Decision Rule			
Power Decision Rule			

Are you satisfied with the way your board uses these rules?

Should the weights be changed?

A Final Perspective on Boardship

"Ooops. The blinking red light means the board of directors is naked in a big pile."

A Final Perspective on Boardship

Overview

Our discussion of boards would be incomplete without some attention to common problems. The issues here focus on moving toward a "better board."

Chapter 19

Toward a Better Board

As must be clear from this manual, boards today face a host of problems. Many of these difficulties can be traced to a lack of preparation and serious concern on the part of the directors, the board's overreliance on the executive, a lack of training and preparation for board roles, poorly developed information bases upon which to make decisions, and excessive fault finding among directors. Boards need a systematic plan of transition.

Transitioning to a Better Board

How does an organization move toward having a better board? Certainly not by simply asserting that things should be "better." Begin by viewing the board as you would any decision-making group, and work to improve the meeting and group decision process. Consider a training session, with a specific training curriculum. As your board's meeting processes improve, directors will be more receptive to spending some time on their specific roles as directors. A follow-up training session on board responsibilities would be appropriate. Developing a manual for board directors could assist the transition. This plan sounds straightforward, but it is really complex and requires a lot of work. Knowing that board meetings can and will improve can sustain and motivate the transition from an administration board to a policy board.

The Problems of Transition

Many a human service organization has been founded by a group of interested citizens who initially get together and are the agency. As time passes, the agency may acquire federal or state moneys. As more stable funding becomes available, the agency hires an executive director and perhaps a secretary. The organization begins to move from a very informal, nonbureaucratic, personal organization to one that is more formal and bureaucratic, with a board of directors legally chartered under the laws of the state. The transition often leaves agency founders feeling left out and like they need to move on.

Founding members tend to be very involved in all aspects of the agency's life. Because they were involved in the organization's founding, they tend to believe and act as if they have special knowledge and wisdom about the direction that the agency should take, the strategic orientation it should demonstrate to the community, and how the agency should operate itself. Further, and again because of their founding roles, they tend to believe that their views should have more weight, that their preferences should dominate. The field of business enterprise is littered with the carcasses of firms and individuals who were unable to make the transition from what Flamholtz [1986] calls an "entrepreneurial" status to a "professional" status.

Because power and influence are not easily given up, new directors recruited to work with founding members often find the job frustrating. Not infrequently, they believe that their own perspectives are not heeded, that board decisions are overturned or sabotaged indirectly, and that initiatives are undertaken without appropriate board consideration. Sometimes, a founding member or members, along with other directors, will hire an executive director, hoping to "professionalize" the administration of the agency. Not infrequently, conflict soon breaks out between the founding members and the executive director. In one case we know of, a new executive director entered his office and discovered a founding member sitting at the new executive's desk, using the new executive's phone. Adding insult to injury, the founding member asked the new executive to wait outside for a few minutes while the founding member finished some business. Such behavior, and the assumptions behind them, are often the sources of trouble and difficulty as the organization grows. Hence, preparation for transition, including a discussion of these very issues, is well advised. One should not expect, however, that this discussion will solve all the problem, but it certainly is a start.

Further Motivation for Change

There is another motivation for board improvement, however, that is more practical than improvement for improvement's sake. The goal of board improvement is better-quality decisions, not just pleasant meetings in which decisions are made. Increasingly, because of pressures for accountability and responsibility, boards are assessed in terms of the quality of their decisions and the processes they use to arrive at those decisions. This trend is beginning now with nonprofit community boards in a number of fields. External reviewers from national agencies, accrediting bodies, funders, and other groups are including board assessments in their review processes. While still not widespread, it is a trend of significant proportions and one that should serve as an important additional stimulus for boards to improve their functioning and the quality of their decisions.

Putting These Tools to Use

Many boards in the nonprofit sector seem to have difficulty carrying out their tasks [Schmid, Dodd, & Tropman 1987]. For this reason, constant review and refurbishment— of board decisions and decision-making processes, of how the board carries out its responsibilities, of how members of the group fulfill their roles, and of how the board conducts its meetings—are necessary. This manual has offered a number of tools that will assist the board in rejuvenating, refurbishing, and redirecting the organization for which it is a trustee.

Appendix
Liability and Risk Management

"*Would everyone check to see they have an attorney? I seem to have ended up with two.*"

Appendix

Liability and Risk Management

Tom A. Croxton[1]

Charitable Immunity

Throughout most of the history of nonprofit, charitable institutions, the doctrine of charitable immunity protected nonprofit organizations from most law suits. When matters related to civil wrongs came up, such as negligence or personal injury, the charity could hide behind the immunity doctrine to escape liability for wrongful acts.

If our legal system still adhered to the doctrine of charitable immunity, little consideration might be afforded to matters related to liability and risk management in a text on nonprofit boards. In large part, however, the immunity of charitable organizations from law suits has been abolished. Although many reasons exist for the demise of this doctrine, including the growth and development of both charities and the insurance industry, the principal rationale was provided by courts of law, which opined that when an innocent victim suffers harm as a result of the conduct of agency personnel, whether they be paid employees

---

[1] Tom A. Croxton, MSW, JD, is a professor at the School of Social Work, University of Michigan. Special thanks to John E. Tropman, who was heavily involved in an early version of this appendix.

or volunteers, the innocent party should have to bear the monetary burden of the injury.

An important point is that the charitable-immunity doctrine protected organizations, not individuals. Although the organization might have been protected from liability by the charitable-immunity doctrine, individuals who worked for the charity, employees and volunteers alike, were not. Ironically, the party with the most resources, the organization, was immune from suit, whereas the parties with the least resources, volunteers, were left with no protection.

Equally ironic is that as judges have abolished charitable immunity for organizations, they have not moved to provide immunity to volunteers, who offer their considerable energies in promoting organizational goals and serving clients free of charge, In other words, the courts did not substitute organizational liability for individual liability. While, as a society, we extol the virtues of volunteerism, encouraging individuals to participate in solving an array of social problems, we provide a considerable disincentive by asking volunteers to open themselves to the risk of personal liability for their conduct. The resulting policy question, quite simply, is: How do we expect people to volunteer services if in doing so they put themselves in jeopardy of being sued?

At the State Level

Some states have answered this question in limited ways. Alabama holds a volunteer who performs services for a nonprofit organization immune from civil liability for good faith acts within the scope of the volunteer's official functions and duties [Code of Alabama 1993]. As in other states, willful and wanton misconduct by a volunteer forms an exception. Colorado has adopted similar language and provides broad immunity to directors acting within the scope of their duties. The Colorado statute makes clear, however, that such immunity does not "diminish or abrogate any duties that the director...has to the nonprofit organization" [Colorado 1996].

Delaware allows an agency's certificate of incorporation to contain or limit the director's personal liability, except for

- breach of loyalty;
- acts or omissions not in good faith;
- intentional misconduct;
- a knowing violation of the law, or any transaction from which the director derives an improper personal benefit [Delaware 1996].

Some states, like Massachusetts, New Hampshire, South Carolina, and Texas place absolute dollar limitations on suits against certain nonprofit corporations. These may be as low as $20,000 in Massachusetts to as high as $1 million in Texas [Nonprofit Risk Management Center 1993, 1995].

But state legislation often comes in bits and pieces, without attention to more comprehensive policies. Some states provide fairly comprehensive protections for charities, while others provide fairly limited immunity. Some states may provide no protective shield. In considering such matters, each organization and each volunteer director must examine the laws of the state in which the nonprofit is incorporated and where it conducts its activities. The best way to discover applicable laws is for the organization to retain an attorney experienced in the law of charitable organizations. The Nonprofit Risk Management

Center in Washington, DC, publishes an updated compendium of state liability laws for charitable organizations and volunteers.[2] The Council of Foundations in Washington, DC, can also be helpful.[3] For individuals contemplating working for charitable organizations as volunteers, whether in direct service or as board directors or trustees, it is imperative that they find out about the extent of their liability for conduct on behalf of their nonprofits.

At the Federal Level

After years of legislative futility, and out of concern about the growing unwillingness of volunteers to offer services in light of legitimate fears about frivolous, arbitrary, capricious law suits and the high cost of liability insurance coverage, Congress passed the Volunteer Protection Act in 1997. This law provides an immunity shield as long as

- the volunteer was acting within the scope of his or her responsibilities;

- if appropriate or required, the volunteer was properly licensed, certified, or authorized by the state for the activities or practices in question;

- the harm was not the result of willful or criminal misconduct or a conscious indifference to the rights or safety of the individual harmed by the volunteer; or

---

[2] Nonprofit Risk Management Center, 1001 Connecticut Avenue NW, Suite 900, Washington, DC 20036; 202/785-3891, fax 202/833-5747; www.nonprofitrisk.org.

[3] Council on Foundations, 1828 L Street NW, Washington, DC 20036; 202/466-6512, fax 202/785-3926; www.cof.org.

- the harm was not caused by the volunteer operating a motor vehicle, vessel, or other craft for which the state requires a license.

The Volunteer Protection Act protects the volunteer, but not the nonprofit organization; nor does it wholly pre-empt state law. Neither does the act relieve board members of their obligations, duties, and responsibilities to the organization.

Fiduciary and Other Duties of Directors

Directors are expected to carry out their duties and obligations to the organization in good faith, with the care a prudent person would apply in the same or similar circumstances, and in a manner the director reasonably believes to be in the best interest of the nonprofit organization. Directors can, of course, rely on the opinions of experts and on reports and statements presented by executive officers or agency committees, unless the individual directors have knowledge to the contrary. This reliance, however, does not relieve directors from three general duties:

- diligence in accomplishing the purposes for which the nonprofit was incorporated;
- avoiding harmful effects that result from their negligence; and
- prudence, good faith, and the avoidance of self-serving or personally enriching conduct

Diligence

The board of directors has a legal responsibility to accomplish the purposes set forth in the organization's articles of incorporation. This kind of accountability is not strictly or tightly defined, but the board can be taken to court if it appears it has failed to accomplish the purposes of the non-profit in substantial ways, or if it has pursued purposes other than those defined by the articles.

As social conditions change and social problems become redefined, nonprofits are asked to respond. Despite perceived needs, the availability of new funding opportunities, or compelling arguments for intervention, the organization should not respond in ways that are outside the parameters of the nonprofit's purpose as articulated in its articles of incorporation or bylaws.

Avoiding Harmful Effects

The board of directors is responsible for conducting the organization's affairs in such a way as to avoid harm to those who come in contact with the agency. Avoiding harm means that the organization's physical plant and service programs must be reasonably safe. In this era of quality assurance, not only must directors of nonprofit organizations attend to their organizations' purposes and policies, but they should insist upon careful monitoring and evaluation of all programs. Directors should also review agency policies and procedures with regard to those who provide direct services, whether they be employees or volunteers.

Some states may protect directors for simple negligence, but none allow statutory immunity for gross negligence. This is one arena in which insurance becomes a must, not only for the organization, but also for directors who may be sued by third parties. It is incumbent on directors to have all insurance policies reviewed to ensure that the extent and amount of coverage is adequate and that policies are up to date in light of current law.

Several forms of liability insurance are available to cover the directors of nonprofit organizations. Directors and officers insurance covers acts deemed to be unreasonable or imprudent. Acts of omission or commission deemed to constitute malpractice may be covered by errors and omissions insurance. Beyond insurance, directors may be indemnified against liability in the nonprofit's articles of incorporation, if allowed by state law. Such indemnification, however, is limited to the assets of the charitable organization, meaning that if the losses are greater than the assets, the individual director may still be held personally responsible.

Prudence and Good Faith

Prudence and avoidance of self-enriching conduct implicates concepts of loyalty, good faith, acting in the organization's best interest, and monitoring and avoiding conflicts of interest. Perhaps the clearest area of board responsibility is avoiding personally enriching conduct. This most directly involves compensation beyond reimbursement for expenses or small honoraria—items such as cash loans or gifts in property from the agency to the director. This standard is frequently applied to any business relationships between directors and the agency.

Conflicts of interest may not always lead to problems, but they can and should be watched carefully. Conflicts occur when a director is involved in a transaction from which he or she derives some personal benefit from what the organization may be doing. In such cases, the director must withdraw from participating in the deliberations or action on the matter. Less clear is the popular practice in which some organizations seek professional opinions, such as legal or fiscal advice, for example, from directors serving on the board. When the board needs such knowledge and skills, it should, as a general rule, seek them from outside the organization, whether it be for hire or pro bono. This does not mean that lawyers or other professionals should not serve on boards. Rather, directors should be appointed in their capacities as citizens instead of as professionals. The dual role of being a director and a disinterested professional is potentially a great source of conflict and mischief.

On occasion, a person may serve on two or more boards simultaneously. Here, conflicts of interest become especially ticklish. If the charitable organizations are in competition for fund raising, programs, grants, or contracts, what the director knows from serving on one board cannot be shared, directly or indirectly, with the other. Serving on multiple boards can place one in a very compromising position, involving vague and uncertain lines between loyalty and disloyalty. Before agreeing to serve on more that one board, one should fully explore the potential conflicts.

The Standard of Care

Directors of nonprofit corporations in New York State are required by statute to discharge their duties in "good faith with the degree of diligence, care, and skill which ordinarily prudent men would exercise under similar circumstances in a like position" [Consolidated Laws 1990]. This is similar to statutory language in other states. The standards of diligence and good faith require considerable interaction between the executive staff and the board so that directors are up to date on purposes, intents, and implications of actions on which they are required to vote. Whatever the knowledge, involvement, or concern of a particular director, that director is legally responsible for the actions of the board unless he or she has statutory immunity. Diligence and good faith require an informed and involved board of directors. Fulfillment of this standard not only requires consistent attendance at board meetings, but also that directors insist on being fully informed on all matters within the parameters of the board's authority. Directors cannot just sit comfortably as figureheads or rubber stamps for executive decisions.

Directors are required to act with the same degree of prudence and judgment in advancing the financial and other business affairs of the organization as they would reasonably do in handling their own personal affairs. There is an objective standard of reasonableness here, so negligence in handling one's personal business affairs does not excuse negligence in handling the organization's business dealings.

Other Legal Responsibilities

Many other points are relevant to the legal responsibilities of volunteers, but these are best left to a nonprofit corporation attorney. The purpose here is alert volunteers to some of the issues they may need to consider. Every board should consult a corporate counsel as soon as possible regarding its liabilities and whether current policies and practices conform to state law. Below are checklists for making choices and minimizing risks that apply to both directors and volunteers serving nonprofit, charitable organizations.

For Directors

❐ Ask for a copy of and carefully read your organization's bylaws. Be clear about the organization's mission. These documents are not the most exciting reading you will encounter, but you should be clear about the purpose and organizational structure of the nonprofit, and the responsibility you undertake in becoming a director. If you do not understand some matters, ask for clarification.

❐ Do not accept a position on the board if you do not take the responsibility seriously. Serving on a board is not a trophy or luxury appointment. It means hard work and dedicated commitment.

❐ Be sure of your motivations for serving on a board. If your primary motivation is to promote your own entrepreneurial and professional advancement, you probably should not accept a board position.

❐ Ask for clarification regarding your liability as a board member. The Volunteer Protection Act focuses primarily on direct service volunteers and does not wholly abrogate state law. Ask for a written legal opinion on state law. Make sure any liability that inheres to board members is adequately covered by insurance.

❐ Attend all meetings if possible. When you cannot attend a meeting, make sure you know what is on the agenda and provide feedback in absentia. The same caution applies to any committees on which you sit. As a general rule, you cannot vote by proxy unless permitted by state law.

❐ Insist that all minutes, reports, or other documents on the agenda are received well in advance of meetings. Nonprofits, like other organizations, have a habit of producing last-minute reports for action by governing boards. Do not accept the "press of time" argument for tardy reports.

❐ Do not go into a board meeting unprepared. Formulate concerns and questions in advance. Make sure that policy decisions are made on the basis of adequate information and are within the guidelines of the articles of incorporation and state and federal regulations, if any.

❐ Always pay close attention to budgetary matters, and be reasonably certain that financial reports contain adequate information. Without access to the budget, a board member can be largely left in the dark about agency priorities, specific program allocations, and money trails. As with many organizations, allocations to cover administrative costs may outweigh moneys directed at service obligations.

❐ Ask to see the agency's conflict-of-interest statement. Many agencies will not have one, but this is a special area of concern for board members. They all have lives outside the boardroom, and they must be clear as to when to withdraw from particular decisions on grounds of conflict of interest.

❐ Do not be overwhelmed by expertise nor fear that asking questions will expose your own ignorance. Be an active participant. Executive officers of nonprofits, like those of for-profit organizations, may prefer to have their way and hope to encounter a rubber stamp board. Do not rely totally on an expectation that organizational executives will always do the right thing.

When Hiring Volunteers

❏ Obtain a careful personal history of each volunteer, including letters of recommendation. In some service programs, especially those dealing with children, a check of any criminal history may be advisable, if not mandated by state law. Checking a person's criminal history can, admittedly, be an expensive inquiry. In an ideal world, this expense should be provided by external sources, such as state government, but the lack of such support is no excuse for not protecting recipients of service.

❏ Volunteers should receive a thorough orientation to the organization, including statements of mission, ethics, rules of conduct, agency policy and procedures, potential liability, and the limits of the organization's insurance coverage.

❏ Volunteers should receive a short course on safety issues, not only for themselves, but for those they serve as well.

❏ The agency should have an established in-service training program for all volunteers.

❏ The agency should take every reasonable means to integrate volunteers into the agency's organizational life.

❒ The organization should have written policies and procedures related to volunteers, including termination of service.

❒ The agency should supervise volunteers with the same care and concern as with paid employees.

❒ The agency should establish a code of conduct for both volunteers and paid employees, including written policies that prohibit sexual harassment and other forms of discrimination.

❒ Volunteers, like employees, should receive annual evaluations, and the agency should establish annual performance awards.

❒ Insurance is a must. Even where laws grant immunity to volunteers, the organization may be found liable. In addition, insurance is necessary to cover those acts of volunteers that fall outside federal or state immunity policy.

Know Your Legal Responsibilities

Knowledge of the legal responsibilities and commitments is one of the director's primary obligations, not only to him- or herself, but also to the organization. Just wanting to "do good" is no long sufficient, if it ever was. Indeed, these matters should be explored before one assumes a directorship or otherwise volunteers for a charitable organization. Similarly, the nonprofit organization itself has some responsibilities that involve the careful orientation and preparation of directors and other volunteers, risk management policies and procedures, and sufficient insurance to protect volunteers against personal loss.

Bibliography & References

Alexander, J.A., & Weiner, B.J. (1998). The adoption of corporate governance model by nonprofit organizations. *Nonprofit Management & Leadership, 8,* 223–242.

Austin, D.M., & Woolever, C. (1992). Voluntary association boards: A reflection of member and community characteristics? *Nonprofit and Voluntary Sector Quarterly, 21,* 181–193.

Axelrod, N.R. (1994). Board leadership and board development. In R.D. Herman (Ed.), *The Jossey-Bass handbook of nonprofit leadership and management* (pp. 119–136). San Francisco: Jossey-Bass.

Bell, P.D. (1993). *Fulfilling the public trust: Ten ways to help nonprofit boards maintain accountability.* Washington, DC: National Center for Nonprofit Boards.

Bradshaw, P.; Murray, V.; & Wolpin, J. (1992). Do nonprofit boards make a difference? An exploration of the relationships among board structure, process, and effectiveness. *Nonprofit and Voluntary Sector Quarterly, 21,* 227–248.

Bradshaw, P.; Murray, V.; & Wolpin, J. (1996). Women on boards of nonprofits: What difference do they make? *Nonprofit Management & Leadership, 6,* 241–254.

Bramson, R.J. (1981). *Coping with difficult people.* New York: Ballentine Books.

Carver, J. (1990). *Boards that make a difference.* San Francisco: Jossey-Bass.

Carver, J. (1996). *Chairperson's role as servant leader to the board.* San Francisco: Jossey-Bass.

Carver, J. (1996). *Planning better board meetings.* San Francisco: Jossey-Bass.

Carver, J. (1996). *Strategies for board leadership.* San Francisco: Jossey-Bass.

Carver, J., & Carver, M.M. (1996). *Basic principles of policy governance.* San Francisco: Jossey-Bass.

Carver, J., & Carver, M.M. (1996). *Your roles and responsibilities as a board member.* San Francisco: Jossey-Bass.

Carver, J., & Carver, M.M. (1997). *Reinventing your board: A step-by-step guide to implementing policy governance.* San Francisco: Jossey-Bass.

Carver, J., & Shrader, A. (1997). *Boards that make a difference: A new design for leadership in nonprofit and public organizations.* San Francisco: Jossey-Bass.

Casey, R.W. (1998). *Best practices for nonprofit boards: Managing finances and investments.* Homewood, IL: Irwin Professional Publishers.

Child Welfare League of America. (1996). *CWLA board self-assessment checklist.* Washington, DC: CWLA Press.

Child Welfare League of America. (1996). *CWLA standards of excellence for the management and governance of child welfare organizations.* Washington, DC: CWLA Press.

Cleese, J. (1988, May 16). No more mistakes and you're through. *Forbes, 141,* 126, 128.

Clifton, R.I., & Dahms, A.A.M. (1980). *Grassroots administration: A handbook for staff and directors of small community-based social service agencies.* Prospect Heights, IL: Wavelin Press.

Code of Alabama. (1993). Vol. 5, Art. 6-5-336. Charlottesville, VA: Michie Co.

Cohen, M.; March, J.G.; & Olsen, J. (1972, March). A garbage can model of organizational choice. *Administrative Science Quarterly, 17*, 1–25.

Colorado Revised Statutes. (1996). 1996 Cumulative Supplement, Title 13, Vol. 6A, Sec. 13-21-115.7(b)(2)(3). Denver: Bradford Publishing Co.

Conrad, W.R., Jr., & Glen, W.E. (1983). *The effective voluntary board of directors.* Athens, OH: Swallow Press.

Consolidated Laws of New York Statutes. (1997). Book 37, Art. 7, Sec. 717. St. Paul, MN: West Group.

Delaware Code Annotated. (1996). Vol. 4, Tit. 8, Sec. 102(d)(7). (1996 Supplement). Charlottesville, VA: Michie Co.

Drucker, P.F., & Rossum, C. (1993). *How to assess your nonprofit organization with Peter Drucker's five most important questions: User guide for boards, staff, volunteers, and facilitators.* San Francisco: Jossey-Bass.

Duca, D.J. (1986). *Nonprofit boards.* Phoenix: Oryx Press.

Duca, D.J. (1996). *Nonprofit boards: Roles, responsibilities and performance.* New York: John Wiley & Sons.

Eadie, D., & Daily L. (1994). *Boards that work: A practical guide to building effective association boards.* San Francisco: Jossey-Bass.

Emenhiser, D.L.; King, D.W.; Joffe, S.A.; & Penkert, K.S. (1998). *Networks, mergers, & partnerships in a managed care environment.* Washington, DC: CWLA Press.

Flamholtz, E.G. (1986). *How to make a transition from entrepreneurship to a professionally managed firm.* San Francisco: Jossey-Bass.

Greenleaf, R. (1973). *Trustees as servants.* Peterborough, NH: Windy Row Press.

Hardy, J.M. (1990). *Developing dynamic boards: A proactive approach to building nonprofit boards of directors.* Erwin, TN: Essex Press.

Hart, P. (1990). *Groupthink in government.* Bristol, PA: Taylor & Francis.

Harvey, J.B. (1974, Summer). The Abilene paradox. *Organizational Dynamics, 63–80.*

Herman, R.D. (1988). *Non-profit board of directors: Analyses and applications.* New Brunswick, NJ: Transaction Publishers.

Herman, R.D.; Renz, D.O.; & Heimovics, R.D. (1997). Board practices and board effectiveness in local nonprofit organizations. *Nonprofit Management & Leadership, 7,* 373–385.

Herman, R.D., & Van Til, J. (1989). *Nonprofit boards and directors: Analysis and applications.* Washington, DC: National Center for Nonprofit Boards.

Houle, C.O. (1989). *Governing boards: Their nature and nurture.* San Francisco: Jossey-Bass.

Ingram, R.T. (1989). *Ten basic responsibilities of nonprofit boards.* Washington, DC: National Center for Nonprofit Boards.

Janis, I. (1972). *Victims of groupthink.* Boston: Houghton Mifflin.

Janis, I. (1983). *Groupthink: Psychological studies of policy decisions and fiascos.* Boston: Houghton Mifflin.

Janis, I., & Mann, L. (1997). *Decision making: A psychological analysis of conflict, choice, and commitment.* New York: The Free Press.

Kaner, S.; Lind, L.; Toldi, C.; Fisk, S.; & Berger, D. (1996). *Facilitator's guide to participatory decision-making.* Branford, CT: New Society Press.

Kluger, M.P., & Baker, W.A. (1994). *Innovative leadership in the nonprofit organization: Strategies for change.* Washington, DC: CWLA Press.

Kluger, M.P.; Baker, W.A.; & Garval, H.S. (1998). *Strategic business planning: Securing a future for the nonprofit organization.* Washington, DC: CWLA Press.

League of Women Voters. (1979). *Simplified parliamentary procedure.* [Pamphlet]. Washington, DC: Author.

Leifer, J.C., & Glomb. M.B. (1997). *Legal obligations of nonprofit boards: A guidebook for board members.* Washington, DC: National Center for Nonprofit Boards.

Levy, L. (1981, January/February). Reforming board reform. *Harvard Business Review, 59,* 166–172.

Margolis, R.J. (1989, September). In America's small town hospitals.... *Smithsonian, 20,* 52–67.

Mintzberg, H. (1994). *The rise and fall of strategic planning.* New York: Free Press.

Moynihan, D.P. (1969). *Maximum feasible misunderstanding.* New York: Free Press.

Murray, D. (1998). *Nonprofit budgeting step by step: A practical workbook for managers and boards.* San Francisco: Jossey-Bass.

Myers, R.J.; Ufford, P.; and McGill, M. (1988). *On-site analysis: A practical approach to organizational change.* Etobicoke, ON: On Site Consultant Associates.

Naisbitt, J., & Aburdene, P. (1985). *Reinventing the corporation.* New York: Warner.

National Information Bureau. (1979). *The volunteer board member in philanthropy.* New York: Author.

Nonprofit Risk Management Center. (1993, 1995). *State liability laws for charitable organizations and volunteers* (2nd edition with 1995 modifications). Washington, DC: Author.

Parkinson, C.N. (1957). *Parkinson's law.* New York: Houghton Mifflin.

Perkins, K.B., & Poole, D.G. (1996). Oligarchy and adaptation to mass society in an all-volunteer organization: Implications for understanding leadership, participation, and change. *Nonprofit and Voluntary Sector Quarterly, 25,* 73–88.

Plous, S. (1993). *The psychology of judgment and decision making.* Philadelphia: Temple University Press.

Portnoy, R.A. (1986). *Leadership: What every leader should know about people.* Englewood Cliffs, NJ: Prentice-Hall.

Schmid, H.; Dodd, P.; & Tropman, J.E. (1987). Board decision making in human service organizations. *Human Systems Management, 7,* 155–161.

Schwarz, R.M. (1994). *The skilled facilitator: Practical wisdom for developing effective groups.* San Francisco: Jossey-Bass.

Sims, R. (1992). Linking groupthink to unethical behavior in organizations. *Journal of Business Ethics, 11,* 651–652.

Stebbins, R.A. (1996). Volunteering: A serious leisure perspective. *Nonprofit and Voluntary Sector Quarterly, 25,* 211–224.

Stein, T.J. (1998). *Child welfare and the law* (Rev. ed.). Washington, DC: CWLA Press.

Stoesz, E., & Raber, C. (1997). *Doing good better! How to be an effective board member of a nonprofit organization.* Intercourse, PA: Good Books.

Tichy, H., & Devanna, M.A. (1990). *The transformational leader.* New York: John Wiley & Sons.

Tjosvold, D. (1986). *Working together to get things done.* Lexington, MA: Lexington Books.

Tropman, J.E. (1984). *Policy management in the human services.* New York: Columbia University Press.

Tropman, J.E. (1995). The role of the board in the planning process. In J.E. Tropman, J. Erlich, & J. Rothman (Eds.), *Tactics and techniques of community practice* (3rd ed.) (pp. 157–171). Itasca, IL: F.E. Peacock.

Tropman, J.E. (1996a). *Effective meetings: Improving group decision making.* Thousand Oaks, CA: Sage Publications.

Tropman, J.E. (1996b). *Making meetings work: Achieving high quality group decisions.* Thousand Oaks, CA: Sage Publications.

Tropman, J.E. (1998). *Managing ideas in the creating organization.* Westport, CT: Quorum Books.

Tropman, J.E.; Johnson, H.R.; & Tropman, E.J. (1992). *Committee management in the human services* (2nd ed.). Chicago: Nelson-Hall.

Tropman, J.E., & Morningstar, G. (1989). *Entrepreneurial systems for the 1990s.* Westport, CT: Quorum Books.

Tropman, J.E., & Tropman, E.J. (1995). Index of dissimilarity and the professional unit method of analysis. In J.E. Tropman, J. Erlich, & J. Rothman (Eds.), *Tactics and techniques of community intervention* (3rd ed.) (pp. 467–470). Itasca, IL: F.E. Peacock.

Public Law 105-19, *Volunteer Protection Act of 1997.* (1997, June 18). 105th Cong., 1st sess.

Waldo, C.N. (1985). *Boards of directors: Their changing role, structure, and information needs.* Westport, CT: Quorum Books.

Widmer, C. (1993). Role conflict, role ambiguity, and role overload on boards of directors of nonprofit human service organizations. *Nonprofit and Voluntary Sector Quarterly, 22,* 339–356.

Wood, M. (Ed.). (1995). *Nonprofit boards and leadership: Cases on governance, change, and board-staff dynamics.* San Francisco: Jossey-Bass.

Zander, A. (1982). *Making groups effective.* San Francisco: Jossey-Bass.

Zander, A. (1993). *Making boards effective.* San Francisco: Jossey-Bass.

Zelman, W. (1977). Liability for social agency boards. *Social Work, 22,* 270–274.

Internet Resources

Council on Foundations ....*www.cof.org*

National Center for Nonprofit Boards .... *www.ncnb.org*

Nonprofit Risk Management Center ..... *www.nonprofitrisk.org*

About the Authors

John E. Tropman is a professor of human services management and organizational behavior at the University of Michigan, Ann Arbor. He coordinates the MSW-MBA program at the School of Social Work and School of Business and serves as faculty associate for the university's program in American Culture. In addition, he teaches in the Executive Education Programs at both the Michigan Business School and Carnegie Mellon University, Pittsburgh, Pennsylvania. He is a lecturer and author and consults with government, nonprofit, and commercial organizations. He received his bachelor's degree in sociology from Oberlin College, Oberlin, Ohio; his master's in social work from the University of Chicago; and his doctorate in social work and sociology from the University of Michigan.

Elmer J. Tropman (deceased) received his master's in sociology and certificate in social work from the University of Buffalo, Buffalo, New York. He served as executive director of the Council of Social Agencies of Buffalo and Erie Counties, New York, and executive director of the Health and Welfare Planning Association of Pittsburgh and Allegheny County. Upon retirement, he developed and directed the Forbes Fund of the Pittsburgh Foundation. His working life emphasized, encouraged, and enhanced human services management.